The Novels of Henry James:

A study of culture and consciousness

The Novels of Henry James:

A study of culture and consciousness

Brian Lee

St. Martin's Press   New York

© Brian Lee 1978

For information, write:
St. Martin's Press, Inc., 175 Fifth Avenue, New York, N.Y. 10010
Printed in Great Britain
Library of Congress Catalog Card Number 78–16902
ISBN 0–312–57969–1
First published in the United States of America in 1978

Library of Congress Cataloging in Publication Data

Lee, Brian.
   The novels of Henry James.
   Bibliography: p.
   Includes index.
   1. James, Henry, 1843–1916 – Criticism and interpretation.
I. Title
PS2124.L36   813'.4   78–16902
ISBN 0–312–57969–1

Contents

Preface

At this time the single most important task for the critic of Henry James is probably that of rescuing the novelist's work from the distorting, Procrustean bed of philosophical theory in which it so uncomfortably rests. No matter whether the particular theory advanced is that of James's father, brother, or even John Locke, the advocates of these various interpretations never fail to do an injustice to the quality of James's art and the nature of the ideas expressed in it. I have tried, therefore, in this study to present James's ideas about the nature of civilization and of the self not as a coherent or precise formula taken over from a modern Aquinas, but as the product of a mind 'so fine that no idea could violate it' – of an intelligence that always maintained its ability to respond freely and openly to new forms of experience. James was subject to certain influences of course, as all artists are, and I have indicated those I consider to be the major ones; but none of these can account for the continuing importance his novels have.

James's vital interests – those which make him something more than a 'thinker' with a secret relation to a body of thought – are those linking his work to that of men like Henry Adams and T. S. Eliot. James's persistent concern to understand the values on which his civilization was based, and his attempt to assess those values, give his work a continuing importance of the kind that is associated with the *Education* say, or with *The Waste Land*, where thinking is creative, not a matter of propagating ideologies but of treating ideas with the respect that the artist owes to them.

Ideas are living things. They do not have an independent, disembodied existence – that goes without saying. Yet artists who treat them as such are rare indeed. James's concern for the individual – for his will and his desires, his 'moral vibrations' and his decisions – was a concern for civilization as a whole, which, he realized, was amply reflected in the small space he chose to illuminate.

His intense preoccupation with the presentation of consciousness grew directly out of this concern, and I have therefore taken pains to attempt a refutation of those critics who see his late manner as a 'hypertrophy of technique'. My extended analysis of the structure and style of *The Ambassadors* is intended to demonstrate the ineluctable connection between form and content, thought and its object, or at its furthest reach the self and its world. It is in the late novels, if anywhere, that James lays claims to be the foremost novelist and the most radical innovator of his age, and it is by the success of these that he must ultimately be judged. *The Portrait of a Lady* is a major masterpiece of nineteenth–century fiction, but coming as it does towards the end of a long European tradition, it is not nearly so impressive an achievement as his later work – the first great fiction of the modern era.

Acknowledgements

A number of institutions and individuals helped me at various stages in the production of this book. The American Council of Learned Societies awarded me a fellowship which allowed a year's uninterrupted work in the Houghton and Widener Libraries of Harvard University. The editors of *Renaissance and Modern Studies* and the *British Association for American Studies Bulletin* published essays which form parts of chapters 7 and 8 and have given permission for their use in this study. Professor Henry Gifford, Dr A. E. Rodway and Mrs Gwen Thiman all gave me invaluable help and encouragement during the research, writing and preparation of my manuscript. I am deeply grateful to them.

1

The education of
Henry James

The most useful advice for anyone wishing to trace James's mental and artistic development is contained in a sentence he wrote himself when preoccupied with the problems of biography and auto-biography: 'To live over other people's lives is nothing unless we live over their perceptions, live over the growth, the changes, the varying intensity of the same – since it was by these things they themselves lived.' The need to 'live over' James's life is amply provided for by *A Small Boy and Others, Notes of a Son and Brother*, and *The Middle Years*, as well as by James's published letters, which render much of the data carefully accumulated by his biographers superfluous. In the realms where James's autobiographies and letters are of little assistance to the critic, biographies are of even less use, and in attempting to assess James's credentials as a critic of his own and comparable cultures one must deal with a background far wider than that provided by the immediate facts of his life and with influences more pervasive and less easily traced than those which he himself tells us about in his three volumes of autobiography.

The central fact from which such an assessment must begin is the fact of his nationality. As James himself said: 'one's supreme relation, as one had always put it, was one's country.' James's relation to America has been the subject of as much discussion as has his relation to Europe. In *The Complex Fate*, Marius Bewley takes as the great American novelists Cooper, Hawthorne, Melville, and James. They are novelists, he says, who are essentially opposed to the frontier tradition of American literature, and who are linked by their common critical consciousness of the national society. They realized both 'the dangers and the deficiencies . . . encircling the possibilities they believed the country possessed' and out of 'the tension between their faith and their fears' sprang 'the best art America has ever produced.'[1] F. R. Leavis in his introduction to *The Complex Fate* agrees in the main with what Mr Bewley says about the American tradition and goes on to add:

1. *The Complex Fate*, by Marius Bewley (London, 1952).

I myself, then, see Mr Bewley as pointing to a major significance that Henry James has for me, a significance bound up with my sense of his greatness. I am thinking of that drama of critical interplay between different traditions which has so large a part in his *oeuvre*. It represents, as I have remarked elsewhere, a comparative enquiry, enacted in dramatic and poetic terms, into the criteria of civilization, and its possibilities.

While it is easy to agree with both Leavis and Bewley it is not because either of them has presented a detailed, convincing argument in support of the views they put forward. Bewley discusses in some detail the influence of Hawthorne on James, confining himself largely to a study of *The Blithedale Romance, The Bostonians, The Marble Faun* and *The Wings of the Dove*; and in *The Great Tradition*, as well as admitting to a 'drastic selectiveness of material', Leavis places James in a different tradition of novelists – one which comprises Jane Austen, George Eliot, Conrad, James and Lawrence – whereas many of the central qualities in James are bound up with what is essentially American in him and which, naturally enough, Leavis ignores. It has been suggested that for James Europe simply represented the past and America the present. It is easy to see how such a view could gain currency. It fits in neatly for instance with a persistent theory that America renews herself culturally with every new generation. But such simplification should not be allowed to obscure the fact that James had a vital connection with the American past – a connection which he could not possibly have had with Europe:

> For the American writer has never (if he is honest and American) been able to pretend an authentic initial communion with the European past . . . .. He can know a great deal, even everything, about that past; he can go after it, which is just the demonstration that he is not in communion with it. And if he establishes communion, it is one of a quite different order from that which most European writers – until 1939 at least – possessed as their birthright.[2]

This is how R. W. B. Lewis puts it in *The American Adam*, where he is attempting to trace the dominant theme in American thought of the nineteenth century as it is crystallized in representative imagery and anecdote. This theme is embodied in the image 'of the authentic American as a figure of heroic innocence and vast potentialities, poised at the start of a new history', and it is worked out in the form of a debate or a Platonic dialogue; though it also lurks, Lewis believes, 'behind the formal structure of works of fiction'. Similar structural or thematic designs have been uncovered in classic American fiction by Tony Tanner in *The Reign of Wonder* and David

---

2. *The American Adam: Innocence, Tragedy, and Tradition in the Nineteenth Century*, by R. W. B. Lewis (Chicago, 1955).

L. Minter in *The Interpreted Design as a Structural Principle in American Prose*. What the precise relations were between nineteenth-century fiction and the nutritive intellectual soil from which it grew is still a matter of debate, but the general connections have been well attested. As for that background itself, the ethical polemics of nineteenth-century American theologians have lost what urgency and appeal they once had and the bitter clashes between the Calvinists of Princeton and Andover, and the New England social reformers are only of interest in so far as they throw some light on the dominant themes in thought and literature.

The simplest formulation of the Adamic myth is probably Emerson's, 'Here's for the plain old Adam, the simple genuine self against the whole world', and in this form it finds its chief prophet in Whitman whose *Leaves of Grass* celebrates a return to the Adamic condition of joyous innocence. The elder Henry James, and indeed many others, found Emerson's enthusiasm naive and unjustified, and there was an attempt to incorporate the Adamic myth into a tragic philosophy for, as James said, 'nothing could be more remote . . . from distinctively *human* attributes . . . than this sleek and comely Adamic condition.' It was the tragedy inherent in the American Adam's innocence which inspired novelists to take up the myth and to enlarge it. Their response took the form of asking: 'Supposing there were such a figure – young, pure, innocent – what would happen if he entered the world as it really is?' And the various answers they gave involved the creation of such characters as Donatello, Pierre, Billy Budd, Daisy Miller, Isabel Archer, Christopher Newman and Huckleberry Finn.

In James's novels the simple dialectic is enlarged and enriched almost beyond recognition. To explain *The Portrait of a Lady* for example, in terms of a clash between innocence and experience is to be guilty of crude over-simplification. What happened to James's Adam is a question to be answered in later chapters, but I am concerned at this point not with James's development of the myth but the source from which he took it. Undoubtedly he was influenced to a great extent by Hawthorne, as Bewley has shown. He was also indebted to his father and I shall examine the nature of that indebtedness. But in the main I agree with Lewis that he got this, his 'most important inheritance from his own culture, . . . where everyone else seemed to be getting it: in the impalpable atmosphere of the time. The myth of the American Adam was simply a formula for the way life felt to alert and sensitive Americans during the second and third quarters of the nineteenth century; it could hardly have been missed by the younger Henry James.'

Henry James's father was born into a Calvinist family against which he soon rebelled, feeling that 'the early development of my moral sense was every way fatal to my natural innocence, the innocence essential to a free evolution of one's spiritual character.' All his life he was to continue a most vehement critic of both moralism and the Church:

> Morality is the summer lustihood and luxuriance of self-love, clothing its mineral ribs with vegetable grace, permeating its rigid trunk with sap, decorating its gnarled limbs with foliage, glorifying every reluctant virgin bud, and every modest wifely blossom into rich, ripe motherly fruit. Religion is the icy winter which blights this summer fertility, which arrests the ascent of its vivifying sap, and humbles its superb life to the ground, in the interests of a spring that shall be perennial, and of autumns bursting with imperishable fruit.[3]

He remained a critic of all institutions, including that most peculiar one: 'the New England conscience, with its fussy self-consciousness and self-culture'. These attitudes are not surprising perhaps in one who considered it the main task of democracy to destroy the established institutions, yet they make a strong contrast with his son's chagrin directed against the 'thinness' of American society:

> No State, in the European sense of the word, and indeed barely a specific national name. No sovereign, no court, no personal loyalty, no aristocracy, no Church, no clergy, no army, no Diplomatic Service, no country gentleman, no palaces, no castles, nor manors, nor old country houses, nor parsonages, nor thatched cottages, nor ivied ruins; no cathedrals, nor abbeys, nor little Norman churches; no great universities, nor Public Schools – no Oxford, nor Eton, nor Harrow; no literature, no novels, no museums, no pictures, no political society, no sporting class – no Epsom nor Ascot![4]

Henry James Senior soon came under the influence of Swedenborg, the mystic, and Fourier, the social reformer, to both of whom he remained an ardent, if somewhat eccentric, disciple. His last major work, *Society: the redeemed form of Man,* is devoted to an attempt to show how Fourier's 'Divine Society' and Swedenborg's 'Grand Man' can be brought into existence. Men, he believed, must cease to believe in independence of the individual and come together in a collective spiritual being. In the pursuit of this ideal James Sr found himself, as I have already said, in opposition to the current hopeful view of man as expressed in the work of Emerson. To the view of the American as Adam he was especially antagonistic. For James, Adam is a 'dull, somnolent, unconscious clod', and R. W. B. Lewis credits him with a more mature attitude towards 'the allegory of every individual's spiritual adventure'. James believed that 'growing up

3. Quoted by R. B. Perry in *The Thought and Character of William James,* vol. I (Boston, 1935).
4. *Hawthorne,* by Henry James (London, 1879).

required the individuating crisis which in Genesis is dramatized as the Fall of Adam: the fatal necessary quickening within the unconscious chunk of innocence of the awareness of self. This egotism and selfhood is essentially sinful and can only be overcome by a second crisis leading to the individual's re-birth as a social being.' This, then, is the Jamesian myth of the Fortunate Fall, and it would be foolish to deny that it bears some similarity to the 'spiritual adventures' undertaken by several of the characters in his son's novels. It is obvious that the novelist is aware of the pattern, even if he doesn't assent to his father's conclusions. At the same time it does not follow that James used his father's philosphy as a skeleton upon which to construct an 'allegory of man' in his late novels. This is the view put forward by Quentin Anderson in his essay 'Henry James and the New Jerusalem'[5] and at greater length in his book *The American Henry James*. It is difficult for any critic of James to ignore these views but whichever position he adopts on them he is likely to find himself hard pressed, for the kind of reasons demanded by either acceptance or rejection of Anderson's thesis are not likely to be forthcoming. And if he attempts to compromise by suggesting that James was probably influenced to some extent by his father's ideas and that some of them found their way unconsciously or consciously into his work he will have an almost equally difficult task in attempting to credit James – a most self-conscious and self-critical artist – with such a seemingly haphazard or unconscious art. Still, a stand has to be taken on this issue for if Anderson is right, the consequences for the study of James and indeed for criticism in general are very far-reaching indeed.

Anderson begins by recalling the way in which Henry James the elder thought the redeemed form of Man could be achieved. First comes 'formation' in which God denies himself in order to distribute 'Divine Love' among other beings besides Himself. Then comes 'creation' making us capable of love. ('Creation' necessarily involves the Creator and obscures his perfection in the exact ratio of its evolving the creature and illustrating his imperfection.) The creature illustrates his imperfection by abandoning the Divine Love and clinging to his selfhood or 'proprium'. Under the influence of his selfhood Man sees the world being full of objects to be grabbed, and feels that his selfhood stands in opposition to Nature or to Divine Wisdom. Not until he rejects this dualism and comes to see the world as a poem describing his own nature has he abandoned the

---

5. Anderson's essay was published in *The Kenyon Review*, Vol. 8, 1946. His argument is developed further in 'The Two Henry Jameses' (*Scrutiny*, Vol. XIV, 1946–7), and 'Henry James, his symbolism and his critics' (*Scrutiny*, Vol. XV, 1947–8). It is most fully articulated in his book, *The American Henry James* (New Brunswick, N. J., 1957).

idea of his separateness; then the third stage, 'marriage', has been reached, and he can be said to be regenerate. Anderson thinks that the way in which James Sr uses these ideas – the limits of identity, and of self-love and love for others – as the forces behind action in the moral sphere, makes him one of the great 'naturalists of the self', and he compares his work to that of Freud, coming to the conclusion, however, that Henry James's theology is a closed world from which we 'step with ease . . . into the closed world of the son's novels.' Whether or not we do in fact step with ease into the 'closed world' of the novels depends partly on our acceptance of Anderson's interpretation of such stories as 'The Real Thing', 'The Jolly Corner' and 'The Figure in the Carpet'. ('It seems plain that the allusion is to the system of the elder James' – plain to Anderson perhaps but not so plain as to prevent at least four other critics from giving a quite different explanation of what that figure is.)[6] But mainly his evidence rests on his interpretation of *The Ambassadors*, *The Wings of the Dove* and *The Golden Bowl*. 'They were', he tells us, 'planned as a single poem embracing the history of mankind. They represent three stages in the experience of the race which are parallelled by three stages in the moral career of the individual', just as these stages are represented in the work of the elder James by three churches – the Jewish Church, the Church of Christ, and the New Church.

Some critics have found this interpretation untenable. I would claim his error is not so much the one of making an entirely false reading of the novels and stories as of vastly over-estimating the degree of James's indebtedness to his father. As Anderson has pointed out himself, 'In the eyes of his best critics James is both a moralist and a symbolist, but has no system of values which relates his morality and his symbols. Some critics, aware that this is an

6. 'The thing which, as it seems to me, James hoped chiefly that his critics would someday recognize is not that he was a great stylist, or a learned historian of manners, or the chief of the realists, or a master of psychological analysis . . .. The thing which he as the high priest selemnly ministering before the high altar, implored someone to observe and to declare is that he adored beauty and absolutely nothing else in the world.' (Stuart P. Sherman in *The Question of Henry James*, ed. by F. W. Dupee, London, 1947).

'His "little trick" was simply not to tell the story at all as the story is told by the Scotts and the Maupassants, but to give us instead the subjective accompaniment to the story.' (J. W. Beach, *The Method of Henry James* (New Haven, 1918).

'He had found – *The Awkward Age* had proved it to him – that a novel might be fundamentally organized. That was the figure in the carpet, that was the joy of his soul; that was the very string his pearls were strung on.' (Van Wyck Brooks, *The Pilgrimage of Henry James* (New York, 1925).

'So it is that James, in himself, is not interesting; he is only intelligent; he has no mystery in him, no secrets; no Figure in the Carpet.' (André Gide in *The Question of Henry James*.)

anomalous situation, admit their puzzlement. Others find James a territory to be occupied – they introduce their own systems as links between James's principles and his art. The artist's artist is asked to shoulder the weight of other men's beliefs.' One is forced to admit the truth of this criticism, whatever doubts one harbours with regard to the particular burden Anderson forces on to James. It remains strange that James himself should fail to make any reference at all to the influence his father's philosophy had on his novels, especially when one remembers that it is just with the genesis of the novels that he is most concerned in the Prefaces.

In *Notes of a Son and Brother*, James has said more about his father's work and the way in which his ideas were treated by his sons. He tells us that:

> They pervaded and supported his existence, and very considerably our own; but what comes back to me, to the production of a tenderness and an admiration scarce to be expressed, is the fact that though we thus easily and naturally lived with them and indeed, as to their more general effects, the colour and savour they gave to his talk, breathed them in and enjoyed both their quickening and their embarrassing presence, to say nothing of their almost never less than amusing, we were left as free and unattached by them, as if they had been so many droppings of gold and silver coins on tables and chimney-pieces, to be taken or not according to our sense and delicacy, that is our felt need and felt honour.

Henry, at least, did not feel the need during his youth to explore his father's theories further. He tells of his 'incurious conduct' with regard to his father's attachment to Swedenborg, and of 'the heroic impunity of my inattention'. Also, whether through modesty, or whether he was merely telling the truth (and if the latter what becomes of Anderson's theory?) he contrasts his own attitude with that of his brother:

> William, later on, made up for this not a little, redeeming so to a large extent, as he grew older, our filial honour, in the matter of a decent sympathy, if not of a noble curiosity: distinct to me even are certain echoes of passages between our father and his eldest son that I assisted at, more or less indirectly and wonderingly, as at intellectual 'scenes', gathering from them the importance of my brother's independent range of speculation, agitations for thought, and announcements of difference, which could but have represented, far beyond anything I should ever have to show, a gained and to a considerable degree an enjoyed, confessedly an interested, acquaintance with the paternal philosophic penetralia.

In his determination to surround his sons with a complete atmosphere of freedom, Henry James applied his ideas to both formal education and formal religion. He had a real hatred of 'forms' and 'institutions', with the consequence that his sons never attended one school or one church with anything approaching regularity. The advantages of the system are obvious when we study the products, though as Henry remarked, 'no education avails for the intelligence that doesn't stir in it some subjective passion, and . . . on the other hand almost everything that does so is largely educative.' Subjective passion certainly served Henry well. If he could only be somewhere 'and somehow receive an impression or an accession, feel a relation or vibration', that for him was enough for 'no particle that counts for memory or is appreciable to the spirit can be too tiny, and that experience, in the name of which one speaks, is all compact of them and shining with them.' The disadvantages of this kind of education are not so obvious and in the end were even turned to advantage in the novels. I have already cited James's lament over the thinness of American society – its inability to furnish the novelist with his essential properties – and one must realize that James was not alone in wishing for a more richly endowed society. Hawthorne knew only too well that 'No author, without a trial, can conceive of the difficulty of writing a romance about a country where there is no shadow, no antiquity, no mystery, no picturesque and gloomy wrong, nor anything but a commonplace prosperity, in broad and simple daylight, as is happily the case with my dear and native land.'[7] And Fenimore Cooper, too, complained of the lack of 'annals, manners and obscure fictions in America'. James though, by virtue of his unique environment, was in some respects even more unfortunately placed in relation to American life. His father, having inherited a considerable income, was never forced into working for a living. He devoted himself exclusively to his various interests and had no contact with the business world whatsoever. This was a source of some embarrassment to his son when he was at school. It was degrading to give the reply 'A student', when asked his father's profession. It was still a source of embarrassment much later, when he wanted to write about American business interests in such novels as *The Ivory Tower*. His father's educational theories, on the other hand, were in part responsible for his belief that American society was even more unvaried and uninteresting than it really was. One has only to read in his autobiography what he has to say about the clergy, for example, to begin to understand some of the views about America and Europe found in the early fiction:

> We knew in truth nothing whatever about them, a fact that, as I recover it, also flushes me with its fine awkwardness – the social scene in general handsomely bristling with them, to the rueful view I sketch, and they yet remaining for us, or at any rate myself, such creatures of pure hearsay that when late in my teens, and in particular after my twentieth year, I began to see them portrayed by George Eliot and Anthony Trollope the effect was a disclosure of a new and romantic species.

7. Preface to *The Marble Faun*.

There were other even more romantic species to be discovered in Europe and it is not surprising that his travels there should play an extremely important part in his education. His first considerable visit began in 1855, but this was not his first exposure to 'that sense of Europe to which I feel my very earliest consciousness waked.' His curiosity had been aroused by his father's English books, and by the European personalities who were frequent visitors to the James household. He had a good opportunity to satisfy his curiosity during the five years between 1855 and 1860 and he informs us in *Notes of a Son and Brother* that 'They had begun, the impressions – that was what was the matter with them – to scratch quite audibly at the door of liberation, of extension, of projection; what they were *of* one more or less knew, but what they were *for* was the question that began to stir, though one was still to be a long time at a loss directly to answer it.' When he returned to Europe in 1869, it was with a much clearer idea of what his vocation was to be. He had already written several stories and had them published in American literary magazines and his interests in European society were now clearly defined. Later still in the salons of Madame Viardot and Madame de Blocqueville, he was to meet Flaubert, Daudet, Maupassant, Zola, Goncourt and Turgenev; and in the midst of this aristocratic society where culture and sensibility were glorified above all he was to be admitted to the 'aristocracy of the fine'. But his real initiation took place on the day he arrived at Liverpool when he was offered the 'extraordinary gage of experience' which he maintained he was never to let drop again. The whole scene is described in *The Middle Years* – the raw March day, breakfast at the Adelphi Hotel:

> 'the damp and darksome light washed in from the steep, black bricky street, the crackle of the strong draught of the British 'sea-coal' fire, much more confident of its function, I thought, than the fires I had left, the rustle of the thick, stiff, loudly unfolded and refolded *Times*, the incomparable truth to type of the waiter, truth to history, to literature, to poetry, to Dickens, to Thackeray, positively to Smollett and to Hogarth, to every connection that could help me to appropriate him and his setting, an arrangement of things hanging together with a romantic rightness that had the force of a revelation.'

Against this feeling of 'romantic rightness', he felt, however, that he must fight if he was to avoid making what he called 'a superstitious valuation of Europe'.

> We are Americans born – *il faut en prendre son parti*. I look upon it as a great blessing, and I think that to be an American is an excellent preparation for culture. We have exquisite qualities as a race, and it seems to me that we are ahead of the European races in the fact that, more than either of them, we can deal freely with forms of civilization not our own, can pick and choose and assimilate and in short (aesthetically, etc.) gain

our property wherever we find it. To have no national stamp has hitherto been a regret and a drawback, but I think it not unlikely that American writers may yet indicate that a vast intellectual fusion and synthesis of the various national tendencies of the world is the condition of more important achievements than any we have yet seen. We must of course have something of our own – something distinctive and homogeneous – and I take it that we shall find it in our moral consciousness, in our unprecedented spiritual lightness and vigour.[8]

This may be taken as James's fictional starting point. It is the expression once more of the Adamic myth. But for him it was only a starting point, and much of the interest lies in seeing how under his care it is varied and developed, probed from every angle, discarded and restored, and finally, in its greatly altered form, incorporated into the whole Jamesion *Weltanschauung*.

8. Letter to T. S. Perry, 20 September, 1867, in *Selected Letters of Henry James*, ed. by L. Edel (London, 1956).

2

Long-haired men and short-haired women

The letter in which James extols the American consciousness was written in 1867, two years before he settled in Europe. His first serious attempt to chart that consciousness and fix it in relation to its native environment was made eleven years later in *The Europeans*. Again in *Washington Square* (1881), and in *The Bostonians* (1886), he returned to the exploration of American society, after which though the international situation occupied the forefront of many novels he came to see it more and more in terms of the complex relationships engendered by the introduction of American individuals into European society until in 1904 he at last revisited America and produced, twenty years after the publication of *The Bostonians*, first *The American Scene*, and finally *The Ivory Tower*,

It is not surprising that for many readers James's early American works represent his best writing. The two earlier books conform exactly to his own ideal for the *nouvelle*:

> . . . the main merit and sign (of the *nouvelle*) is the effort to do the complicated thing with a strong brevity and lucidity – to arrive, on behalf of the multiplicity, at a certain science of control.[1]

and *The Bostonians* remains not only one of the best novels ever devoted to the delineation of American society but also one of the most subtle explorations of the submerged energies and passions which mould and direct that society; executed with an economy that flatly contradicts any but the most superficial relationship to Daudet's *Évangeliste*, or any of the 'loose, baggy monsters' of Naturalism, and with an intelligence that makes the majority of psychological novels seem naïve to a degree.

In this chapter I shall be concerned to trace James's changing attitudes to, and his assessments of the 'unprecedented spiritual lightness and vigour' of Americans which he so valued in 1867. They are reflected throughout by subtle shifts of emphasis and gradual changes in the scope of his critical irony.

1. Preface to *The Lesson of the Master*. James's prefaces are collected in *The Art of the Novel*, ed. by R. P. Blackmur (New Yor, 1934).

James called *The Europeans* a 'sketch', and in a letter to his brother William he admits that it is 'thin' and 'empty'. But he also warns his brother against 'taking these things too rigidly and unimaginatively – too much as if an artistic experiment were a piece of conduct, to which one's life were somehow committed.'[2] He thus disclaims any ultimate responsibility for the attitudes and values stated or implied either by individual characters in the book or by the book as a whole. As to the first – those judgements and views expressed by the characters in the novel – we must, in this book at least, allow him his claim. In *The Europeans* James does not use the 'device' of seeing his story 'through the opportunity and sensibility of some more or less detached, some not strictly involved, though thoroughly interested and intelligent, witness or reporter', who, in later novels often comes to voice views very like those we know James to have held. Every character in *The Europeans* possesses a different viewpoint none of which is shared by James yet out of which he achieves a kind of synthesis which sets before us some at least of the conditions he then thought necessary for an ideal civilization.

Ezra Pound accused James of beginning his career 'with a desire to square all things to the ethical standards of a Salem mid-week Unitarian Prayer Meeting.' In other words he maintains that ultimately James does give his assent to the attitudes propagated by such characters as Mr Wentworth who, in *The Europeans*, is the living embodiment of those New England virtues and vices in question. Perhaps, as Pound says, it takes an American to appreciate the authenticity of such a character, but it does not take an American to see that James is far too critical to give him his unqualified approval. If one has read discriminately, giving due attention and weight to the nuances of James's irony then it should be apparent that he is only too well aware of the deficiencies of puritanism as it is represented by Mr Wentworth. Take for example this comment, made by Felix Young on the Wentworth family:

'It's primitive; it's patriarchal; it's the *ton* of the Golden Age.' (40)[3]

The criticism is dramatized. It characterizes Felix as well as the Wentworths. It depends for its effects on the tone in which it is uttered and on the circumstances which provide the occasion for it; yet it also functions as a descriptive element in James's own picture of New England society.

Perhaps the easiest way to define the differences existing between say, Felix on the one side and Mr Wentworth on the other, is to say that for Mr Wentworth life is approached as a discipline – a

---

2. *The Letters of Henry James*, ed. by P. Lubbock (London, 1920).
3. For the various editions of James's works to which page numbers refer, see Bibliographical Note.

discipline which if it does not allow for the full application of one's talents, at least prevents one from making a wrong application of them. For Felix, life presents an unlimited opportunity – either for success or failure. It is the thought of possible failure, that is the making of mistakes, that prevents Mr Wentworth from taking any enjoyment from his relations with others:

> If you had been present, it would probably not have seemed to you that the advent of these brilliant strangers was treated as an exhilarating occurrence, a pleasure the more in this tranquil household, a prospective source of entertainment. This was not Mr Wentworth's way of treating any human occurrence. A sudden irruption into the well-ordered consciousness of the Wentworths of an element not allowed for in its scheme of usual obligations, required a readjustment of that sense of responsibility which constituted its principal furniture. To consider an event, crudely and baldly in the light of the pleasure it might bring them, was an intellectual exercise with which Felix Young's American cousins were almost wholly unacquainted, and which they scarcely supposed to be largely pursued by any such human society. The arrival of Felix and his sister was a satisfaction but it was a singularly joyless and inelastic satisfaction. It was an extension of duty, of the exercise of the more recondite virtues. (51)

The advent of the Europeans, as far as the Americans are concerned, is in every way beneficial inasmuch as they help to bring about several very important changes in their lives. But apart from Gertrude, who is never in sympathy with the Puritan ethos anyway, it is doubtful if any of them are made to extend their sympathy to any alien form of life. We are told that Mr Wentworth comes eventually to listen for the sound of Gertrude's gaiety; but apart from this, and in one other surprising respect, he remains convinced of the overall superiority of American morals, manners and institutions. His one lapse occurs during the conversation with Felix when he is suddenly impressed by his nephew's worldliness:

> Felix had a confident, gaily trenchant way of judging human actions which Mr Wentworth grew little by little to envy; it seemed like criticism made easy. Forming an opinion – say on a person's conduct – was with Mr Wentworth a good deal like fumbling in a lock with a key chosen at hazard. He seemed himself to go about the world with a big bunch of these inefficient instruments in his girdle. His nephew, on the other hand, with a single turn of the wrist, opened any door as adroitly as a house thief. (93)

Here the reader may find himself asking whether or not Mr Wentworth is right to envy Felix his facility in making moral judgements. It is true that the old man is lacking in experience and that his judgements therefore are not based on a wide enough knowledge of human behaviour. But if they were, would they be thereby any easier to make? His seriousness in this context is to be admired, and any adverse criticism is here aimed at Felix, as may be seen in James's choice of the analogy of a house thief. In another connection altogether we are invited to laugh at Mr Wentworth's all-pervading puritanism. Felix asks him if he may make a sketch of his head:

> 'I should like to do you as an old prelate, an old Cardinal, or the Prior of an Order.'
> 'A prelate, a Cardinal?' murmured Mr Wentworth. 'Do you refer to the Roman Catholic priesthood?'

It is a tribute to the way James has handled Mr Wentworth, that one can detect the horror in his voice as he makes this reply. And it is confirmed a few lines further on:

> 'I think sitting for one's portrait is only one of the various forms of idleness. Their name is legion.' (69)

The definition of a Puritan as one who renounces the life of the flesh in favour of the life of the spirit fails to do justice to the extremism of Mr Wentworth. His renunciation is more complete, so that he habitually withdraws himself from the possibility of any new experience. The resulting isolation is a not uncommon phenomenon in nineteenth-century America, associated both with New England Puritanism and also with the 'Genteel Tradition' which it favoured. Here he is expressing typical caution in the face of 'peculiar' influences:

> 'You must be careful', he said, 'you must keep watch. Indeed we must all be careful. This is a great change; we are to be exposed to peculiar influences. I don't say they are bad; I don't judge them in advance. But they may perhaps make it necessary that we should exercise a great deal of wisdom and self-control. It will be a different tone.' (55)

Yet in spite of the old man's shortcomings, James's treatment of Mr Wentworth is more sympathetic than some of the above illustrations may indicate. The New England brand of Puritanism may not be conducive to much pleasure, ('amuse ourselves? – we are not children') yet when one considers their obvious virtues: their goodness, honesty, nobility, their own particular refinement, one is made aware that in any product of James's civilization these are the basic characteristics which may be supplemented but not superseded. They are characteristics which reappear in Charlotte, Mr Brand and Clifford Wentworth. Clifford, though, is more materialistic. He has about him a slight sense of a new, developing society, anti-pathetic to the Genteel Tradition to which his family belongs:

And in fact, Clifford's ambition took the most commendable form. He thought of himself in the future as the well-known and much liked Mr Wentworth of Boston, who should, in the natural course of prosperity, have married his pretty cousin, Lizzy Acton; he should live in a wide-fronted house, in view of the common; and should drive, behind a light waggon, over the damp Autumn roads, a pair of beautifully matched sorrel horses. Clifford's vision of the coming years was very simple; its most definite features were this element of familiar matrimony and the duplication of his resources for trotting. (113)

Clifford Wentworth would have been contemporary with Abel Gaw in The Ivory Tower. Both are made the subject of James's irony, yet how differently his irony operates in the two books!

The irony is also operative in connection with Robert Acton, another New Englander, but one who has been away from America long enough to be able to be a little more objective in his criticisms of the society to which he has returned. There is something slightly comic though in his view of himself as a man of the world.[4] He is rather, as Eugenia says, 'a man of the Chinese world'. His visit to China does not have any real civilizing influence on him, partly because the American and Chinese cultures do not, for him, imply any important criticism of each other, and he remains almost as provincial as the others:

> Acton had seen the world, as he said to himself; he had been to China and knocked about among men. He had learned the essential difference between a nice young fellow and a mean young fellow, and he was satisfied that there was no harm in Clifford . . . . Of course there was the great standard of morality, which forbade that a man should get tipsy, play at billiards for money, or cultivate his sensual consciousness. (114)

It is surprising that Eugenia should contemplate marrying him, and inevitable that she should eventually decide that

> the conditions of action on this provincial continent were not favourable to really superior women. The older world was, after all, their natural field. (175)

But in the last analysis this must be taken as a criticism made by James, not Eugenia, of European civilization. It is apparent to him that both Americans and Europeans could and should profit greatly by furthering their contacts with each other. It is no less apparent though, that it is the Americans and not the Europeans who are the more likely to do so. And this by 'taking possession' of our past in a

---

4. In his essay, 'The Novel as Dramatic Poem III, *The Europeans*' (*Scrutiny*, Vol. XV, 1947–8), F. R. Leavis suggests a completely different view of Robert Acton. He maintains that 'there is nothing narrow, provincial or inexperienced about Acton's morality', and that 'his valuations have a peculiar authority.' It seems to me that the sentences I have quoted are meant to illustrate just that narrowness which is a feature of the New England ethos described.

way that is impossible for the European himself. As T. S. Eliot has said:

> It is the final consummation of an American to become, not an English-man, but a European – something no born European, no person of any European nationality, can become.[5]

Eugenia's failure in America – and we are left in no doubt that she *has* failed – is not meant to illustrate the aridity of the American social scene so much as the rigidity of European society and the dangers inherent in it. These take the form of social practices every bit as restrictive and inimical to the development of a full, free life, as are the moral taboos of Puritan New England. James expatiates on them, however, in such novels as *The American*, and they will be dealt with along with James's other early 'European' novels.

Writing to W. D. Howells in 1880, James felt obliged to take up at some length Howells' protest 'against the idea that it takes an old civilization to set a novelist in motion':

> It is on manners, customs, usages, habits, forms, upon all these things matured and established, that a novelist lives – they are the very stuff his work is made of; and in saying that in the absence of those 'dreary and worn-out paraphernalia' which I enumerate as being wanting in American society, 'we have simply the whole of human life left' you beg (to my sense) the question. I should say we had just so much less of it as these same 'paraphernalia' represent, and I think they represent an enormous quantity of it.

Later in the same letter he tells Howells that he has written 'a poorish story in three numbers – a tale purely American, the writing of which made me feel acutely the want of the paraphernalia.' James was always to maintain his poor estimate of *Washington Square*, even to the extent of omitting it from the New York edition of his collected works, and one can only wonder at his blindness to the merits of this penetrating study of the 'best society' of mid-century New York.

Washington Square suggests a comparison with a novel like Edith Wharton's *The Age of Innocence* and to put these two side by side may help to define more clearly James's essential superiority, which is indicated by saying that it consists in his ability to transcend the limits set by the novel of manners in a way that was beyond the capabilities of even such a gifted novelist as Edith Wharton.

The Age of Innocence describes the pressures brought to bear by New York society in the nineteenth century on two of its members engaged in an illicit love affair. In the name of good taste the lovers are forced to separate and to return to their petty, meaningless

5. 'On Henry James in Memory' in *The Question of Henry James*.

routines. Edith Wharton's detailed satire of the society is magnificent. Operas, balls, engagement rites, the ceremonies of dining – all are minutely described with keen, ironic observation; thus creating the atmosphere in which a small, closed, ingrown and completely artificial community once had its being – 'a small and slippery pyramid, in which, as yet, hardly a fissure had been made or a foothold gained.' At the apex of this pyramid, living in a 'super-terrestrial twilight' were the three families which alone could claim an aristocratic origin:

> the Dagonets of Washington Square, who came of an old English county family allied with the Pitts and Foxes; the Lannings, who had intermarried with the descendants of Count de Grasse; and the van der Luydens, direct descendants of the first Dutch governor of Manhattan, and related by pre-revolutionary marriages to several members of the French and British aristocracy. (*The Age of Innocence*, 42)

It is as though a tiny fragment of the European aristocracy had been transplanted and allowed to continue its ritualistic, ceremonial way of living, completely divorced from the environment in which it evolved. And as such it does not provide an effective answer to James's complaint about the lack of manners, usage and custom in America. The society described in *The Age of Innocence* was a feature of the American scene, but it was not an American phenomenon. On the other hand, the distinctly American flavour of *Washington Square* cannot be mistaken. The opening pages with their description of Dr Sloper evoke a milieu subtly different from that of *The Age of Innocence*:

> In a country in which, to play a social part, you must either earn your income or make believe that you earn it, the healing art has appeared in a high degree to combine two recognized sources of credit. It belongs to the realm of the practical, which in the United States is a great recommendation; and it is touched by the light of science – a merit appreciated in a community in which the love of knowledge has not always been accompanied by leisure and opportunity. It was an element in Dr Sloper's reputation that his learning and his skill were very evenly balanced; he was what you might call a scholarly doctor, and yet there was nothing abstract in his remedies – he always ordered you to take something. (17)

The movements which disturb the tranquility of the social scene are observed from a viewpoint somewhat removed from Edith Wharton's – one which takes account of the underlying parochialism and the naïve vigour of polite society – as for example in the following speech:

> 'That's the way to live in New York – to move every three or four years. Then you always get the last things. It's because the city's growing so quick – you've got to keep up with it. It's going straight up town – that's

where New York's going. If I wasn't afraid Marion would be lonely, I'd go up there – right to the top – and wait for it.' (37)

The difference I am attempting to define between the two novels consists in this: whereas Edith Wharton's satire is directed at the formal rites and social observances as such, James is concerned to isolate a peculiarly American quality that has been imposed upon those rites; and in doing so he is led to examine the more fundamental characteristics of American civilization and to make these the subjects of his novel. As he said in his letter to Howells, manners are important inasmuch as they 'represent' life. The mistake made by the novelist of manners is to forget this representative aspect, and to treat manners as having only an intrinsic value. In *The Age of Innocence* manners are an index to nothing beyond themselves; in *Washington Square*, to the moral climate in which they have their origin.

For his 'centre' in *Washington Square*, James chooses a young, plain girl, Catherine Sloper, whose 'spiritual lightness' places her in the tradition of Jamesian heroines. Like the Countess Olenska's in *The Age of Innocence*, her love affair is frustrated by pressures brought to bear from outside, but not in Catherine's case by

> people who dreaded scandal more than disease, who placed decency above courage, and who considered that nothing was more ill-bred than 'scenes' except the behaviour of those who gave rise to them. (*The Age of Innocence* 266)

It is Catherine's father, Dr Sloper – 'that perfect embodiment of the respectability of old New York' – who exposes the venality of Catherine's suitor and effectively condemns her to a life barren of meaning or happiness, passed in the observance of the trivialities of the routine existence:

> There was something dead in her life, and her duty was to try and fill the void. Catherine recognized this duty to the utmost; she had a great disapproval of brooding and moping. She had, of course, no faculty for quenching memory in dissipation; but she mingled freely in the usual gaieties of the town, and she became at last an inevitable figure at all respectable entertainments . . . . She developed a few harmless eccentricities; her habits, once formed, were rather stiffly maintained; her opinions, on all moral and social matters, were extremely conservative; and before she was forty she was regarded as an old-fashioned person, and an authority on customs that had passed away. (174)

Where she differs from Milly Theale or Isabel Archer is in her lack of beauty, grace, or exceptional intelligence. 'Catherine was decidedly not clever', nor, James tells us, had anyone 'ever thought of regarding her as a belle'. Later James will develop the American girl into an 'heiress of all the ages', and later still in his last incomplete novel, *The Ivory Tower*, turn back to his original conception of her; and indeed there is a fittingness in Rosannah Gaw's similarity to Catherine Sloper – a significance bound up with his fluctuating estimates of America's possibilities. For a somewhat different approach to the problems of American civilization we must now look more closely at *The Bostonians*.

James's concern with the representative aspect of manners and customs has already been noticed. He had the remarkable gift of being able to present a microcosm, sometimes in a single character, of a whole society or culture, and had little need to resort to the massive documentation of a Zola or a Dos Passos. *The Bostonians*, however, stands somewhat apart from the main body of his work by the very fact that here he succeeded in writing a novel which ultimately depends on the factual knowledge he undoubtedly possessed relating to New England society in the 1870s. He wished, he says, to write a very American tale, and this is just what *The Bostonians* is. It is realistic in a way that none of his other works, especially the European ones, ever could be. Every last detail both about individuals and of society as a whole is confirmed by everything we know about the history of Boston. He tried to do the same kind of thing for London society in *The Princess Casamassima*, and did it well enough to convince Lionel Trilling that the book is 'grainy and knotted with practicality and detail'.[6] It will not be difficult to prove that this is not the case in fact and that Professor Trilling conforms to his own example of the foreign critic who is not sufficiently attuned to an alien society to recognize its genuine 'hum of implication'. The same problem hardly arises with *The Bostonians*. One has only to recall the indignation which greeted the book's appearance in America to feel reassured that James had accurately taken the measure of polite Boston society and that his portraits are not distorted.

The Bostonians then, has a unique place in James's work, in that more than any other novel it allows James to be quite explicit in his analysis of a very important section of American society. It must not be thought, though, that its importance as a social document is incommensurate with its merits as a work of art. *The Bostonians* is one of the masterpieces of American literature. Dealing with a provincial subject the book yet remains free from the arid provincialism that dogs so many nineteenth-century American novels. It is a witty, mature work – the product of a sensibility which, though sympathetic to the New England culture, is yet sufficiently enlightened to see it as it appears in the light of an older and richer civilization. There is about *The Bostonians* a complete sureness of touch – a confidence which is lacking in the early European novels.

6. *The Liberal Imagination* (New York, 1950).

Consider for example two characters who are in every respect comparable. Amanda Pynsent of *The Princess Casamassima* is adequate to the uses James puts her to, but only just. She hopes for and dreams of an aristocratic future for Hyacinth Robinson in the same way that Miss Birdseye in *The Bostonians* dreams of a future in which women will finally attain their true place in society. Both characters provide him with material for brilliant, sustained irony; yet in the case of Pinnie, the London dressmaker, there is missing that 'solidity of specification' which makes Miss Birdseye such a concretely realized figure. Miss Pynsent is such that she is neither fully representative nor yet particularly individual. Miss Birdseye, on the other hand, on her very first appearance reveals to us a whole new world:

> In her faded face there was a kind of reflection of ugly lecture lamps; with its habit of an upward angle, it seemed turned towards a public speaker, with an effort of respiration in the thick air in which social reforms are usually discussed. (36)

Her representative character, however, did not prevent her from being recognized by many Bostonians as a portrait of Miss Peabody, Hawthorne's well known reforming sister-in-law, and James, as we shall see, went to considerable lengths to refute the charge.

Comparisons like this can be multiplied throughout James's early work and they throw an interesting light on his contention that the texture of American life was too thin to provide a sufficient ground for the novelist. Nevertheless such evidence as this cannot be used to bolster the chauvinistic criticism which castigates James as an expatriate who would have done better to remain at home and cultivate 'an authentic American consciousness', for, as has been pointed out, the standards which enable James to place so accurately such people as Miss Birdseye are not those of Boston nor even can they be called American at all. If *The Bostonians* is a great work of American fiction it is because, paradoxically, its author had become something more than an American novelist.

R. B. Perry in his book on William James says that the

> Transcendentalists, Brook Farmers, and Romantic Humanitarians, were William James's spiritual uncles. They belonged definitely to the past, and were already beginning to wear the aspect of historic monuments. Although being reared with a wise tolerance and liberality, he suffered no reaction against the associations of his youth; these men of his father's circle influenced him congenitally, rather than as contemporary and living forces.[7]

Henry James too felt the influence of these 'spiritual uncles' but his

7. *The Thought and Character of William James*, by R. B. Perry.

reaction to them was more ironic. He came to think of them as 'long-haired men and short-haired women . . . a great irregular army of nostrum-mongers, domiciled in humanitary Bohemia', and he obviously has some sympathy with the people who saw them as 'witches and wizards, mediums and spirit-rappers and roaring Radicals'. The mushroom growth of reforming societies between 1840 and 1850 was the natural outcome of the optimism which pervaded American society in the nineteenth century. Typical of the spirit informing such bodies is the following notice which appeared in 1847:

> Notice is hereby given to all men and women that a Convention of Reformers, who are willing to become the Messengers of Jesus Christ, for the introduction of the New Era of Universal Peace among all mankind, will be held at the Trumbull Phalanx (situate in Trumbull County, Ohio, nine miles west of Warren, and five miles north of the village of Newton Falls) to commence its sessions on the 12th Aug. next 1847, for the purpose of instructing and initiating them in the points which must be made manifest before the Millennial Dispensation of Good Will and Universal Peace amongs all mankind will be established upon the earth in accordance with the express design and guidance of the Spirit of God.
>
> Andrew B. Smolnikor
> (Formerly R. C. Priest and Professor of Divinity – now Messenger of the Dispensation of the Fullness of Time. Ephesians 1–10)[8]

This is 'Frogpondium' at its worst. Miss Birdseye, who belonged to the Short Skirts League as a matter of course, and every League which had ever been founded for almost any purpose whatever, is typical of the average reformer. Anyone sympathetic to the aims of Abolitionism, say, was almost sure to have similar feelings towards the Free Soil Movement, The Peace Society, the Owenite Movement and Transcendentalism. As Emerson, who himself had a tenuous connection with the Brook Farm experiment, said: 'In the history of the world, the doctrine of reform had never such scope as at the present hour . . . . We are to revise the whole of our social structure, the State, the school, religion, marriage, trade, science, and explore the foundations in our own nature.' James's own father was the most ardent of Swedenborgians, and also a convinced Fourierite. His book *Society: the Redeemed Form of Man* is an exposition of his whole system, and he spent his time when not writing, lecturing throughout New England on such topics as 'The Social Significance of our Institutions'. His system, part mystical, part socialist, was treated with affectionate amusement by his family. But although neither William nor Henry could accept their father's doctrines they never ceased to respect his intellect; and Henry writing to his brother about the elder James's last book recalls

8. Quoted by R. B. Perry.

how intensely original and personal his whole system was . . . . I can't
enter into it (much) myself – I can't be so theological nor grant his
extraordinary premises, nor throw myself into conceptions of Heavens
and Hells, nor be sure that the keynote of Nature is humanity etc. But I
can enjoy greatly the spirit, the feeling and the manner of the whole thing.

This indicates as well as anything how Henry James might have been
expected to react to the whole tenor of Boston society with which he
inevitably associated his father and his contemporaries. There is
irony certainly – it is implicit on every page of *The Bostonians* – but
it is not entirely free from a nostalgia for the crude energy and
earnest zeal of the New England reform movement, for the expanded
moral consciousness which he felt to be lacking in Europe. Bearing
this in mind, one feels that Olive Chancellor's thoughts were not
described with only an ironic intent, but that they contained an
important element of truth for James himself:

> It struck Miss Chancellor that this frumpy little missionary was the last
> link in a tradition, and that when she should be called away – the heroic
> age of New England life – the age of plain living and high thinking, of
> pure ideals and earnest effort, of moral passion and noble experiment –
> would effectually be closed. (162)

Whatever his opinions there is no doubt that he was able to back
them with a mass of factual knowledge gained by first-hand experience, and it is true to say that the characters in *The Bostonians* are as
representative of American democracy as any that have appeared
before or since in American fiction. They are every bit as revealing as
De Tocqueville's uncanny generalizations in *Democracy in America*,
and they have the advantage of being better presented. It must not
be thought though that James had brought off a lucky hit. He had
been working towards this consummation for years, and every
character in *The Bostonians* has its first faint origins in an earlier
work. A long procession of more or less well defined Americans
including Daisy Miller, Henrietta Stackpole, Mrs Hudson, Christopher Newman, Mr Wentworth contribute to the success of Miss
Birdseye, Verena Tarrant, Matthias Pardon, Olive Chancellor, Basil
Ransome and Selah Tarrant. A lot has been written about the
dependence of *The Bostonians* on Hawthorne's *Blithedale Romance*,
but such a dependence is in most respects superficial and it would be
far more worth while to examine the use James makes of his own
early experiments in *The American*, *The Europeans*, and *The Portrait
of a Lady*, when he comes to write this – his American master-piece.

When William James complained that the portrait of Miss
Birdseye was a 'bad business', Henry was at first appalled. He hotly
replied that she 'was evolved from my moral consciousness, like
every other person I have ever drawn', and he was upset to think that

she should be taken for 'a portrait from life'. On reflection though, it seemed to him that: 'if I have made my old woman live it is my misfortune, and the thing is doubtless a rendering, a vivid rendering of my idea,' and he concludes that though she is a subordinate figure, 'she is, I think, the best in the book.' There is a lot to be said for this view, and it is something to do with the fact that 'she was heroic, she was sublime, the whole moral history of Boston was reflected in her displaced spectacles.' In a single sustained image James has somehow managed to recreate the whole ethos of mid-century Boston, and the flavour of the political movements which so agitated it at the time. She is pathetic, grotesque, picturesque and simple-minded, and so too are the '*ci-devant* transcendental tendencies' she represents. It is easy to see why William James thought the business of Miss Birdseye bad. After all, at the time of writing his letter he had read only the first instalment of the serialized book, and had he been able to read the whole thing he would probably have agreed with Henry when he claimed she is 'treated with respect throughout, and every virtue of heroism and disinterestedness is attributed to her.' This is true. Although she is pathetic and ineffectual, and a target for James's satire, she yet represents all that is best in the reform movement in contrast to such figures as Matthias Pardon, Selah Tarrant, even Olive Chancellor, who in various ways demonstrate how such seemingly disinterested aims can be pursued for reasons that are anything but disinterested.

Throughout his life, James never missed an opportunity to satirize American newspapers and newspaper men. It can partly be explained by his own unsatisfactory relationship with certain American periodicals and his contempt for their depressingly low standards. But it also constitutes a deeper criticism of one of the inevitable concomitants of democratic societies — mass communication. De Tocqueville, in his defence of newspapers, contends that not only do they serve to maintain freedom, but that they 'maintain civilization, being the only way in which the exertions of one can be united to the exertions of all the others. He admits that

> in democratic societies newspapers often lead the citizens to launch together into very ill-digested schemes; that if there were no newspapers there would be no common activity. The evil which they produce is therefore much less than that which they cure.[9]

James took an opposite view, and deeply resented the intrusions which the Press made into an individual's private life, not to mention the hypocrisies indulged in on behalf of 'The Public'. Matthias Pardon epitomizes all that is worst in democratic institutions:

9. *Democracy in America*, by Alexander de Tocqueville (New York, 1945).

He had a sort of enamel of good humour which showed that his indelicacy was his profession; and he asked for revelations of the *vie intime* of his victims with the bland confidence of a fashionable physician enquiring about symptoms. (129)

The following interview, which is too protracted to quote in full, has about it the bitterness of caricature. Matthias Pardon is attempting to extract from Mrs Luna the kind of details 'the Public likes', about Verena Tarrant:

'Really, sir, I don't know, and I don't in the least care; I have nothing to do with the business!' Mrs Luna cried angrily.

The reporter stared; then, eagerly: 'You have nothing to do with it – you take an unfavourable view – you protest?' and he was already feeling in a side pocket for his notebook. . . . Mrs Luna sank into the nearest chair, with a groan, covering her face with her hands.

'Heaven help me. I am glad I am going to Europe.'

'That is another little item – anything counts' said Matthias Pardon making a rapid entry in his tablets . . . . Mrs Luna sprang up again, almost snatching the memoranda out of his hand.

'If you have the impertinence to publish a word about me, or to mention my name in print, I will come to your office and make such a scene!'

'Dearest lady that would be a godsend!' Mr Pardon cried enthusiastically. (362)

Though there is no prototype for him in James's novels, Selah Tarrant comes close to being an archetypal figure in American fiction – a type frequently encountered in the work of Faulkner, Sinclair Lewis, Dos Passos, and Steinbeck. Like Tarrant, his successors are often a strange mixture of trickster and spiritual fanatic. De Tocqueville encountered the type – more especially in the Mid-West – and had nothing but praise for this wild spiritualism often bordering on religious insanity:

Is it not wonderful if in the midst of a community where thoughts turn outwards, a small number of individuals are to be found who turn their looks to Heaven?

Such an observation as this seems effectively to mark the difference between De Tocqueville and James. The question about people who turn their eyes to Heaven is irrelevant to the question of fanaticism, and James unlike De Tocqueville refused to be taken in by its particular manifestations.

The brilliance and wit with which James handles these peripheral figures in *The Bostonians* is perfect and his fine presentation of them is better than anything he had achieved of this type before. The treatment of Olive Chancellor is no less perfect but here the excellence is of a different kind. It constitutes a penetrating study of renunciation and self-immolation – traits which are deeply rooted in the New England consciousness and which demand, therefore, serious and painstaking analysis. James begins to probe the psychological basis of Olive's puritanism early in the book. We are told that: 'The most secret, the most sacred hope of her nature, was that some day she might have such a chance, she might be a martyr and die for something.' We are thus prepared for the fulfillment of her desires in her relationship with Verena Tarrant. Verena's response to the plea that they should 'renounce, refrain, abstain' was to wonder 'what could be the need of this scheme of renunciation'. She is the typical Jamesian innocent, ruthlessly cultivated as a vehicle for the feminist movement; and her connection with it is 'the most unreal, accidental, illusory thing in the world'. Her fickleness towards the cause, and the final rupture between the two women afford Olive a great deal of suffering, but, 'The prospect of suffering was always, spiritually speaking, so much cash in her pocket', and she freely avails herself of this supply in the closing scenes of the book. Typically enough she spares herself no degradation and goes off to face the hisses and boos of the great disappointed audience in the Boston lecture hall like 'some feminine firebrand of Paris revolutions erect on a barricade, or even the sacrificial figure of Hypatia whirled through the furious mob of Alexandria.'

By the very skilful way in which he juxtaposes the private and public themes, James contrives to lay bare the relationship between the feminist movement and the psychology of its members – demonstrating truths which strike us as commonplace, but which were considered startling, if not ridiculous, in a world which had not experienced the Freudian revolution. On other aspects of the problem – for instance on the effect of democratic institutions on the equality of the sexes – he is not so explicit. De Tocqueville is quite clear in his view that the great social changes would eventually make women the equal of men but not, he adds, in the way that some people have understood the term. Women must never be allowed into business or politics but must fulfil their own particular nature in the best possible manner. Nothing could be worse, he says, than giving men and women the same functions, imposing on both the same duties, and granting to both the same rights. The only result that this could have would be to make weak men and disorderly women. Nevertheless he mentions that if he were asked to what the singular prosperity and growing strength of the Americans ought mainly to be attributed, he would reply; 'To the superiority of their women.'

These views are just those of Basil Ransome in *The Bostonians*, and we are not at all surprised to discover that De Tocqueville is his favourite author. Even his smugness and complacency are a reflection of the Frenchman's, and James seems to be fully aware of a petty, genteel conservatism. Though James himself avoids these dangers, he does share the belief in the moral superiority of American women, coupled with an equally strong conviction of the inherent social inequality of the sexes. He displays it in his obvious satisfaction in the scene at Mr Burrage's where:

> His guests sat scattered in the red firelight, listening silent in comfortable attitudes; there was a faint fragrance from the burning logs, which mingled with perfume from Schubert and Mendelssohn; the covered lamps made a glow here and there, and the cabinets and brackets produced brown shadows out of which some precious object gleamed – some ivory carving or cinquecento cup. It was given to Olive, under these circumstances to surrender herself, to enjoy the music, to admit that Mr Burrage played with exquisite taste; to feel as if the situation where a kind of truce. Her nerves were calmed, her problems – for the time – subsided. Civilization under such an influence appeared to have done its work; harmony ruled the scene; human life ceased to be a battle. She went so far as to ask herself why one should have a quarrel with it; the relations of men and women in that picturesque setting, had not the air of being internecine. (140)

The dichotomy between the social or the aesthetic on the one side and the moral on the other reaches right to the heart of the Jamesian dialectic. His mind ranges continually between these opposing terms, and any civilization, he intimates, has got to assess correctly the relative merits of the moral and the aesthetic consciousness. In *The Bostonians*, however, the issue tends by the very nature of the theme to be overlaid by other concepts, and it is at two of these that we must finally look.

Nowhere in the novel does James formulate a specific disagreement with De Tocqueville's contention that there is an extreme at which freedom and equality could meet and blend; but the point is made none the less. The whole tenor of the book suggests that Verena Tarrant gained her freedom by marrying Basil Ransome at the expense of equality, and that this freedom is ultimately the more valuable. As W. H. Auden has defined it:

> The real issue has been obscured . . . by the historical struggle for social equality which made liberty seem the virtue – or licence the vice – of which equality was the prized or detested precondition . . . .. An America which does not recognize the difference between equality and liberty is in danger, for, start with equality in order to arrive at liberty, and the moment you come to a situation where inequality is, or seems to you, rightly or wrongly a stubborn fact, you will come to grief.[10]

This is the best general summary of James's own criticism – perhaps one of the most trenchant ever made of American democracy.

10. Introduction to James's *The American Scene* (New York, 1946).

3

Innocents abroad

In a letter to his brother of 1888, James insisted that his eventual aim was to write in such a way that

> it would be impossible for an outsider to say whether I am at a given moment an American writing about England or an Englishman writing about America.

In the three novels about to be discussed there is a gradual progression towards that ideal. *Roderick Hudson* (1876) and *The American* (1877), while asserting the supremacy of American values, yet attempt to convey James's own delight in the possibilities suggested by European civilization. His delight is mingled, of course, with an awareness of the dangers involved in total submission to the corrupt and corrupting beauty of old-world forms; and it is true that the dangers rather than the possibilities occupy the foreground of his two earlier novels making for occasional lapses into romantic melodrama, as for example in his presentation of the French aristocrats, the Bellegardes, in *The American*. With the publication of *The Portrait of a Lady* (1881), however, James achieved a new poise which enabled him to balance critically and objectively the claims of rival cultures. If, to use Edmund Wilson's crude formulation, 'America gets the best of it', it is not, in this novel at least, because he has failed to do justice to the European values.

Some years ago, in *The Cambridge Journal* there was a dispute between Alwyn Berland and G. H. Bantock on the subject of the relationship of morals to civilization in James's novels. The two critics arrived at conclusions which were diametrically opposed, yet their arguments are equally plausible. I reproduce below a short extract from Bantock's article which makes both their positions clear;

> It is not, it seems to me, 'civilization' in its 'formal' or 'aesthetic' sense that in James''s novels 'redeems' people or 'helps to redeem them from their own worst possibilities'; and Mr Berland is misleading when he asserts that 'civilization imposes a set of measurements (or conventions) by means of which our moral sense may function and arrive at values;

manners point to morals, conduct in its everyday social sense, to conduct in its ethical Arnoldian sense.' Admittedly James presents the 'forms' and 'conventions' as vitally important aspects of 'experience'; yet the typical Jamesian moral consciousness exists precisely by rejecting the various social proprieties by which it is surrounded. Far from manners pointing to morals, morals are nearly always shown as standing over against, if not in active antagonism to, manners.[1]

It is obvious that they are arguing at cross purposes. Bantock provides an excellent summary of the theme of the early 'European' novels. But he does not take into account the fact that James himself is not always satisfied with the state of affairs he describes in them. James has an ideal of civilized behaviour which, while not explicitly defined, is hinted at in the characters of Roland Mallet, Ralph Touchett, and in the aspirations of Isabel Archer. And this ideal corresponds more closely with Berland's views.

To make the point in a different way one can find the same arguments rehearsed by L. H. Myers – one of the most underrated of modern English novelists. The following is from *Strange Glory*:

> History, tradition, culture are all very well in their way; but they are not enough. What is history but the story of poor little men like ourselves? I want a vision of man. When I look into the past I see a procession of people in fancy dress – the human spirit taken in by its own various make-beliefs. From that point of view there is very little to choose between the painted savage and Beau Brummel in satin. Manners maketh Society not Man.

What the cahracter wants is 'fullness of life' – 'to throw off the shams and trivialities that cramp and still life.' It is this 'fullness of life' that Isabel Archer is constantly striving for, and like Myers's character she finds that history, tradition and culture are not sufficient in themselves. Whether the choice she makes at the end of *The Portrait of a Lady* is consonant with this fullness of life, or whether she turns her face against it by renouncing its possibilities is a question which must be answered in its proper place. The important thing is to know what the ideal involves, and to see how James progresses towards it.

In the Preface to *Roderick Hudson*, we are presented with a catalogue of faults which James's critical eye easily detected when he came to re-read this, his first novel. In the first place the action is in one part telescoped into a few months when it would have been more credible had it been spread over a corresponding number of years. Secondly he felt that he failed in the early chapters successfully to

---

1. G. H. Bantock, 'Morals and Civilization in Henry James' (*The Cambridge Journal*, Vol. VII, 1953). Berland's essay, 'James and Forster: the morality of class' is published in Vol. VI, 1952.

tackle Northampton, Mass., his 'small square patch of the American scene'; and that the New England girl, Mary Garland, who figures in these early chapters, is rendered insufficiently attractive, so that Roderick's proposal to her, and Roland Mallet's falling in love with her constitute a 'deep damage to verisimilitude'. One can accept these strictures, and even add to them, and still remain convinced that *Roderick Hudson* is essentially a good novel. A certain amount of technical awkwardness can be expected in a first novel and is easily forgiven, especially when, as is the case here, it is overshadowed by the richness and complexity of the subject. This complexity derives not so much from the stringing together of a multiplicity of themes, but rather from the careful analysis of a single situation in all its various aspects. Admittedly the analysis is neither as penetrating nor as objective as it was later to become, but the interests themselves are well defined, and display a maturity to which the great majority of novelists never attain. When he does fail in objectivity, it is because he still feels himself very much an American fighting against a 'superstitious valuation' of Europe, and consequently he sometimes fails to allow the European values their full weight. This American bias manifests itself in unexpected places. For example, in Chapter 3, after Roland has persuaded Mrs Hudson that the best thing for Roderick would be to leave America for Rome, he is given a soliloquy in which the irony of the rest of the chapter is dropped and replaced by a serious note of doubt:

> There seemed to Roland something solemn in the scene in which he had just taken part. He had laughed and talked and braved it out in self-defence; but when he reflected that he was really meddling with the simple stillness of this small New England home and that he had ventured to disturb so much living security in the interest of a far-away fantastic hypothesis, he gasped, amazed at his temerity . . . . As he looked up and down the long vista and saw the clear white houses glancing here and there in the broken moonshine, he could almost have believed that the happiest lot for any man was to make the most of life in some such tranquil spot as that. Here were kindness, comfort, safety, the warning voice of duty, the perfect absence of temptations. And as Roland looked along the arch of silvered shadow and out into the lucid air of the American night, which seemed so doubly vast, somehow, and strange, and nocturnal, he was moved to feel that here was beauty too – beauty sufficient for an artist not to starve upon it.(58)

This belief is one that James always cherished and often reiterated. He often returns to the subject in his letters:

> Looking about for myself, I conclude that the face and nature of civilization in this, our country, is to a certain point a very sufficient literary field. But it will yield its secrets only to a really grasping imagination.

It puts in doubt, though, the validity of the basic premises in *Roderick Hudson*. He tells us in the Preface that he wanted the image of a 'perfectly humane society', yet incapable of providing for art, from which the young sculptor of genius can be transplanted to the society of Europe – a society quite capable of providing for his artistic development but one which is also capable of undermining his moral security.

These two themes, the artists's aesthetic development and his moral decay, provide the central preoccupation of the book and are a key to everything in it. His careful analysis does not, however, detract from the urgency with which the problem is presented and *Roderick Hudson* has a vitality sometimes lacking in the more finely constructed later works where so much is made to subserve the demands of structure. James in his early work is more concerned with 'the spiritual facts' than with the picturesque correspondence they bear to the images he uses to convey them. His symbolism, though often crude, is never fortuitous, and probably affords the best approach to his essential interests.

In *Roderick Hudson* the problem is easily solved, by having for his protagonist an artist whose works and whose attitudes to other works of art provide a ready made symbolic commentary on his total attitudes and actions. And it is the same with the other characters, some of whom are artists, and all of whom freely express their opinions on works of art.

The conflicting aspirations and ambivalences of the nineteenth century American artist soon maninfest themselves in Roderick. One of his early works, *'Thirst'*, represents a youth who is 'innocence, health, strength, curiosity – a lot of grand things', drinking from a cup 'knowledge, pleasure'. He repudiates this thirst, though, in one of his conversations with Roland, declaring that he was

> above all an advocate for American art. He didn't see why we shouldn't produce the greatest works in the world. We were the biggest people and we ought to have the biggest conceptions. The biggest conceptions, of course, would bring forth in time the biggest performances. We had only to be true to ourselves, to pitch in and not be afraid, to fling imitation overboard and fix our eyes upon our National Individuality. (29)

This speech could almost be taken as the credo of the American novelist obsessed with the idea of producing the Great American Novel. But Roderick is easily prevailed upon to relinquish his hopes of becoming the 'typical, original, aboriginal, American artist' when Roland offers to take him to Rome. However, his idealism remains at first unimpaired by his contacts with Europe and he produces two finely idealized works. Typically enough, they represent Adam and Eve!

Sooner or later James has to introduce some values which can serve as antitheses to Roderick's idealism, and be connected exclusively with Europe. When he does so in Chapter 4 they serve not only in 'placing' Roderick: they also place James himself. In this important chapter James introduces Gloriani, a cynical, worldly sculptor of the 'sophisticated school', who attempts to shake Roderick in his boundless idealism. The incident is worth quoting from at length because, by the tone of the whole discussion, James indicates his belief that the faith and vigour of the American more than compensate for his naïvete, and that the sophistication and cynicism of Gloriani are symbols of a civilization that is effete, exhausted and decadent. Roderick has just entered an Arnoldian debate by declaring himself a Hellenist rather than a Hebraist and Gloriani replies:

> 'There is no use trying to be a Greek. If Phidias were to come back he would recommend you to give it up – he'd send you about your business. I'm half Italian and half French, and as a whole, an abandoned cosmopolite. What sort of Greek should I be?'

Roderick, however, persists with his idea:

> 'We stand like a race with shrunken muscles, staring helplessly at the weights our forefathers easily lifted. But I don't hesitate to proclaim it – I mean to lift them again! I mean to go in for big things; that's my notion of my art. I mean to do things that will be simple and sublime.'

And later in the same strain:

> 'I mean to do the Ocean and the Mountains, the Moon and the West Wind. I mean to make a magnificent image of my Native Land.'

He remains perfectly at ease despite Gloriani's predictions:

> 'You'll have at any rate to take to violence, to contortions, to romanticism in self-defence.'
> 'My colossal *America* shall answer you.'

Throughout this exchange Roderick is seen as the

> . . . beautiful image of a genius which combined beauty with power. Gloriani with his head on one side, pulling his long moustache like a genial Mephistopheles and looking keenly from half-closed eyes at the lighted marble, represented art with a mixed motive, skill unleavened by faith, the mere base maximum of cleverness . . . . In all this Roderick's was certainly the *beau rôle*. (99–108)

For all that, Gloriani is right when he says that such idealism as Roderick's cannot be maintained. His next work, after his dissipated holiday in Baden, marks a chnage in his vision. But as well as being an accurate forecast of Roderick's future as an artist, Gloriani's prophecy holds good of the American ideal in general as it came to be treated by novelists like Dos Passos, Hemingway, Fitzgerald and Saul Bellow. Their Adamic heroes, like Roderick, come to be romaticized. In order that they should fly they too must take to violence and contortions.

It would, though, be a gross misrepresentation of *Roderick Hudson* if one were to insist solely on the fatal effect of European experience on American innocence. James is always aware of the dangers for others inherent in Roderick's particular blend of innocence and egotism. And though he does not go to the same lengths in this direction as Dos Passos in *Most Likely to Succeed*, or Graham Greene in *The Quiet American* ('God save us always from the innocent and the good.'), he certainly maintains a degree of critical detachment. It is this detachment that accounts for the biting irony in his portrait of Mr Leavenworth, and the more gentle irony directed against Barnaby Striker and Miss Blanchard. He is better with these latter characters – that is, when he is more sympathetic. In the case of Leavenworth one feels that James is only too conscious of a native tendency to pedantry and moralism which can best be got over by what is almost caricature. Leavenworth is a wealthy American, 'eager to patronize our indigenous talent', who commissions Roderick to make him a representation, in pure white marble, of the '*Idea of Intellectual Refinement*'. James's treatment has an edge of bitterness which had disappeared by the time he created Mr Wentworth of *The Europeans* and Henrietta Stackpole in *The Portrait of a Lady:*

> As a liberal customer, Mr Leavenworth used to drop into Roderick's studio to see how things were getting on and give a friendly hint or exert an enlightened control. He would seat himself squarely, plant his gold-topped cane between his legs, which he held very much apart, rest his large white hands on the head, and enunciate the principles of spiritual art – a species of fluid wisdom which appeared to rise in bucketfuls, as he turned the crank, from the well-like depths of his moral consciousness. His benignant and imperturbable pomposity gave Roderick the sense of suffocating beneath an immense feather bed, and the worst of the matter was that the good gentleman's placid vanity had a surface from which the satiric shaft rebounded. (235–6)

One can hardly expect to extract from this, his first novel 'a moral and a lesson and a consecrating final light'; and yet there is, as Leavis has pointed out, '. . . a glimpsed ideal . . . at the centre of James's preoccupations'. The nearest approach to this ideal is made not in Roderick's idealized sculptures, but in a series of conversations between Roland Mallet and Mary Garland in which he returns to the theme of moral and aesthetic value – saying in effect that one must form the necessary basis of the other, and that a preoccupation with either on its own is bound to be disastrous:

> 'We shouldn't be able to enjoy, I suppose, unless we could suffer, and in anything that's worthy of the name of experience – that experience which is the real taste of life, isn't it? – the mixture is one of the finest and subtlest.' (401)

Roderick's failure consists in the perfect separateness of his sensibility. He never sees himself as part of the whole. His failure to retain his moral integrity in the face of experience leads inevitably to his corruption. This is the general pattern of the early novels. The 'aesthetic forms' of European civilization remain appearances only, masking evil and immorality, and the great problem for the individual is to accept the forms whilst rejecting the substance. Only thus can he retain his 'unspotted brightness'.

On re-reading *The American*, after a number of years, James concluded that:

> The content and the 'importance' of a work of art are in fine wholly dependent on its *being* one: outside of which all prate of its representative character, its meaning and its bearing, its morality and humanity, are an impudent thing.[2]

It is with *The American* as a work of art that criticism must come to terms. And though its success or failure must be discussed in terms of its representative character, its meaning and its bearing and its morality and humanity, to discuss these things in the abstract would be, as James says, an impudent thing.

One is bound to agree with James's own judgement that what he has given us in *The American* is 'arch-Romance' – experience that is not regulated by our sense of the way things really happen. If he had known more about American businessmen and European aristocrats, the alignment of good and evil in the book would not have been so obviously Manichean. He would have realized that Newman's moral innocence was incompatible with his background, and that the Bellegardes' crude wickedness was also incompatible with theirs. As it is the book appears naïve at the level of plot and action and fully merits Leavis's harsh judgement. It is, he says, 'romantic, unreal and ridiculous'.[3]

But there is nothing ridiculous in James's idea of the conflict between the forces represented on one side by the moral consciousness, and on the other by the social consciousness. Or in his conclusion that, with the world ordered as it is, such conflicts are not capable of resolution – the only possible victory being the rather

2. Preface to *The American*.
3. *The Great Tradition* (London, 1951).

hollow one of renunciation. No one can be satisfied by the way in which such ideas are worked out in *The American,* yet if we ignore for the moment the melodramatic and romantic plot, there are plenty of hints in the book of the complex organization and economic selection of materials that characterize James's more mature work.

The task he sets himself is that of comparing Newman's moral spontaneity with the restrictive and dehumanizing effect of social pressures and also, though this engages him to a lesser degree, with the equally restrictive effect of a 'stuffy, New England conscience'. To this end he introduces several minor characters and incidents, which for the humour, economy and penetrating insight of their presentation alone make the book worth reading. As so often in the early fiction the periphery of the novel has much more vitality and verbal animation than the centre. When Newman is travelling around Europe visiting four hundred and seventy churches, admiring the streetcars, and wondering whether or not it would be possible to 'get up' a Gothic tower in San Francisco, he meets a young Unitarian minister who is also making the Grand Tour:

> Poor Mr Babcock was extremely fond of pictures and churches, and carried Mrs Jameson's works about in his trunk; he delighted in aesthetic analysis, and received peculiar impressions from everything he saw. But nevertheless in his secret soul he detested Europe, and he felt an irritating need to protest against Newman's gross intellectual hospitality. (65)

He eventually decides to leave Newman and writes him a letter setting forth his reasons: 'I have a high sense of responsibility. You appear to care only for the pleasure of the hour.' Newman can offer no answer to this charge, so instead he sends to Babcock an ivory statuette representing a gaunt ascetic-looking monk, in a tattered gown. Through the rents of this gown, however, a fat capon could be glimpsed tied to the monk's waist. James says of it:

> Did it mean that he was going to try to be as high-toned as the monk looked at first, but that he feared that he should succeed no better than the friar, on a closer inspection, appeared to have done? It is not supposable that he intended a satire on Babcock's own asceticism for this would have been a truly cynical stroke. (70)

And yet, to be consistent, although he cannot attribute such motives to Newman, the cynicism is nevertheless intended. It is typical of the American Puritan's response to European civilization that he should be both attracted and repelled – attracted by the forms of civilization, and repelled by the impurity on which it is based. Newman on the other hand with his fine moral awareness

> . . . had not only a dislike, but a sort of moral distrust, at uncomfortable thoughts, and it was both uncomfortable and slightly contemptible to feel

obliged to square oneself with a standard. One's standard was the ideal of one's own good-humoured prosperity, the prosperity which enabled one to give as well as take. To expand without bothering about it – without shiftless timidity on one side, or loquacious eagerness on the other – to the full compass of what he called a 'pleasant' experience. (62)

This passage might almost be describing Isabel Archer in the early part of *The Portrait of a Lady*.

At the other extreme, Newman's ability to 'see the crooked from the straight at a glance', enables him to know Noemie Nioche for what she is – a greedy adventuress; a revelation denied to Valentin de Bellegarde with his well integrated sensibility. Here are two typical conversations between them:

'But she has wonderfully pretty arms.'

'But she is a vulgar little wretch, all the same,' said Newman.

'Yes, the other day she had the bad taste to begin to abuse her father, to his face, in my presence.'

'Why she cares no more for her father than for her doormat,' said Newman.

'Oh, that's another affair; she may think of the poor old beggar what she pleases. But it was low in her to call him bad names; it quite threw me off.' (217)

And later when Valentin has engaged himself in a duel on Noemie's behalf, Newman again asserts his sense of the superiority of human values over the meaningless convention that lacks a basis of moral conviction. He regards the duel as 'd . . . . . . d, barbarous and d . . . . . . d corrupt', and Valentin can only reply:

'It is our custom, and I think it is a good thing. Quite apart from the goodness of the cause in which a duel may be fought, it has a kind of picturesque charm which in this age of vile prose seems to me to greatly recommend it. It is a remnant of a higher-tempered time; one ought to cling to it. Depend on it, a duel is never amiss.' (231)

All these touches go into the making of a character who has 'done something and is something', who has not 'stupefied himself with debauchery, nor mortgaged his fortune to social convenience' – a character who needs a better world than this to use his advantages. In the final analysis though, Newman's qualities are not sufficient. In him James has had a very brief glimpse of an ideal, but not one capable of withstanding a close critical scrutiny. If the idealizing commentary is ignored one is forced to see that Newman's personality has too much in common with that of Leavenworth in *Roderick Hudson*. And it is not until he comes to write *The Portrait of a Lady* that James creates a character who can be said to be 'superior' in her own right.

Everything he wrote before *The Portrait of a Lady* seems to be leading up to and is included in that work, but not only included; everything is 'placed' with an unerring rightness. The values he has been weighing against one another in the earlier novels are here done full justice, and though he does tip the scales in the same direction as before, one has the feeling that now he knows better why he does so. He has taken the measure not only of Madame Merle and Gilbert Osmond, but also of Lord Warburton and the English aristocracy; and what is perhaps more important still, he has come to grips with Mrs Touchett, Henrietta Stackpole and Caspar Goodwood.

The centre of James's drama, however, is located in Isabel Archer's consciousness and it is with her that criticism must begin. Isabel is something more than merely another 'American Girl' – a more finely realized Daisy Miller. Here James is staking a real superiority for American values, and he does so far more successfully than in any other of his early novels. So confident is he of Isabel's chances of attaining a 'completed consciousness', which in her is largely bound up with images of a moral nature, that he makes no more attempt to minimize her deficiencies than George Eliot did with her prototype Dorothea Brooke:

> Altogether, with her meagre knowledge, her inflated ideals, her confidence at once innocent and dogmatic, her temper at once exacting and indulgent, her mixture of curiosity and fastidiousness, of vivacity and indifference, her desire to look very well and to be if possible even better, her determination to see, to try, to know, her combination of the delicate, desultory, flame-like spirit and the eager and personal creature of conditions; she would be an easy victim of scientific criticism if she were not intended to awaken on the reader's part an impulse more tender and more purely expectant. (53)

Her determination to see, to try and to know, attracts her towards European civilization, yet her moral integrity guarantees her immunity. We recognize James's own dilemma here, and in Isabel's rejection of Warburton, his implicit recognition of the impossibility of reconciling his conflicting attitudes towards Europe. If she is to pursue her policy of 'expansion', she can only do so satisfactorily in Europe. Gardencourt, the symbol of country-house civilization with its rich perfection,

> . . . at once revealed a world, and gratified a need. The large low rooms, with brown ceilings and dusky corners, the deep embrasures and curious casements, the quiet light on dark, polished panels, the deep greenness outside, that seemed always peeping in, the sense of well-ordered privacy in the centre of a 'property' – a place where sounds were felicitous though accidental, where the tread was muffled by the earth itself and in the thick mild air all friction dropped out of contact and all shrillness out of talk – these things were much to the taste of our young lady. (56)

Yet she has been made aware of the ugliness and misery upon which this social system is based, and also of Warburton's incongruous radicalism:

> 'Their radical views are a kind of amusement; they've got to have some amusement, and they might have coarser taste than that. You see they're very luxurious, and these progressive ideas are about their biggest luxury. They make them feel moral and yet don't damage their position.' (77)

There is more to Isabel's relationship with Warburton than this though. Marriage with him would represent an escape – a separation from the 'usual chances and dangers, from what most people know and suffer'. Such a marriage, with its ease and comfort, would necessitate a renunciation of her ultimate moral responsibilities. When she finally rejects Lord Warburton after meeting him again in Rome, she explains to Ralph Touchett that Gilbert Osmond's overriding advantage lies in his appeal to her 'one ambition – to be free to follow a good feeling'. Lord Warburton's strength and power would deny her the exercise of that freedom, as would Caspar Goodwood's. Osmond's 'very poverties, dressed out as honours' constitute a large part of his attraction for Isabel. This problem can be seen as part of a larger one which occupies James's attention throughout the whole book: the possibility of freeing moral choice from the pressure of one's conditioning. Isabel Archer believes in an inescapable destiny which is predetermined by her particular upbringing and environment, yet she insists on accepting full responsibility for the consequences of her actions.

F. R. Leavis, discussing *Daniel Deronda* in *The Great Tradition* finds *The Portrait of a Lady* lacking in moral substance. He finds fault with James for freeing Isabel Archer from the economic and social pressures which force Gwendolen Harleth's choice, and then demanding uncritical homage and admiration for her when all the time we ought to be blaming her for ignoring the advice of Mr Touchett, Ralph Touchett and Lord Warburton. On the contrary the admiration and homage James tries to exact are entirely her due; more so indeed than in Gwendolen Harleth's case where the economic and social pressures do, despite what Leavis says, mitigate our critical response. By freeing Isabel from these external pressures, James makes her final choice even more praiseworthy. Especially since she has every excuse for evading this responsibility, as Caspar Goodwood points out in his last interview with her:

> 'Why shouldn't we be happy when it's here before us, when it's so easy? I'm yours for ever – for ever and ever. Here I stand, I'm as firm as a rock. What have you to care about? You've no children; that perhaps would be an obstacle. As it is, you've nothing to consider. You must save what you can of your life: you mustn't lose it all simply because you've lost a

part . . .. I swear as I stand here, that a woman deliberately made to suffer is justified in anything in life – in going down into the streets if that will help her! I know how you suffer and that's why I'm here. We can do absolutely as we please; to whom under the sun do we owe anything? What is it that holds us; what is it that has the smallest right to interfere in such a question as this?' (643)

This appeal, which she resists only by making the supreme effort of her life, clarifies her decision: 'She had not known where to turn; but she knew now. There was a very straight path.' Surely Isabel's integrity, preserved in the face of such great provocation does not, if we are making the correct responses, make for moral incoherence in the book. It can be argued that the actual choice she makes is wrong – that she has the wrong conception of where her duty lies. But even this argument is untenable, as I propose to show.

This discussion has taken us too far ahead, and we must now return to Isabel's attempts to come to terms with European civil-ization, which she does only by what seems like an act of rational-ization. It is not that her moral sensibility is submerged under an aestheticism like Osmond's, but that the 'moral retreat' she has hitherto found necessary when confronted with declarations of love from Warburton and Osmond is no longer needed in view of her changed ideals: 'The desire for unlimited expansion had been succeeded in her soul by the sense that life was vacant without some private duty that might gather one's energies to a point . . . . She could surrender to Osmond with a kind of humility, she could marry him with a kind of pride: she was not only taking, she was giving.' (381–2) It may be thought that this decision denotes puritanism far more deeply rooted than is displayed by any of James's conventional puritans in the novel, and that eventually it is detrimental to the 'personal life' and 'completed consciousness' she wishes to cultivate. But what must be insisted upon here is Isabel's reaction to the European's preoccupation with the 'world' and with 'things'. This comes out best in one of her conversations with Madame Merle. Madame Merle speaks first:

'When you've lived as long as I you'll see that every human being has his shell and you must take the shell into account. By the shell I mean the whole envelope of circumstances. There is no such thing as an isolated man or woman: we're each of us made up of some cluster of appurte-nances. What shall we call our 'self'? Where does it begin, where does it end? It overflows into everything that belongs to us – and then it flows back again. I know a large part of myself is in the clothes I choose to wear. I have a great respect for things! One's self – for other people – is one's expression of oneself: and one's house, one's furniture, one's garments, the books one reads, the company one keeps – these things are all expressive . . . ..'

'I don't agree with you. I think just the other way. I don't know whether I succeed in expressing myself, but I know that nothing else expresses me. Nothing that belongs to me is any measure of me: everything's on the contrary a limit, a barrier, and a perfectly arbitrary one.' (216)

What we are presented with by Madame Merle represents the real sterility of European civilization; sterile because the moral sensibility abdicates in favour of the aesthetic, and, paradoxically, because of a morbid preoccupation with 'self', totally unlike Isabel's healthy introversion. These defects show themselves most clearly in Gilbert Osmond, who lives exclusively for the aesthetic value of 'forms', when he has no conception of the values underlying them. This is the basic situation behind much egotism, where the egotist must depend entirely on the people and things which he despises so much. In analysing Osmond's egotism James writes what is, is, in his own words, ' . . . obviously the best thing in the book'.[4] At this point he is most closely engaged with his subject for he is also defining the limitations and shortcomings of a whole society.

It remains only to discuss James's concern with what he calls 'the dusky old-world expedient' of renunciation, and this brings us back to the opening remarks of this chapter on the significance of Isabel's choice in returning to Osmond. It is plain that her moral integrity at least must be granted, but James insists that the reader be prepared to go beyond this and accept that her decision implies neither renunciation nor defeat. Isabel herself realizes that:

Deep in her soul – deeper than any appetite for renunciation – was the sense that life would be her business for a long time to come. (612)

And this is made even more explicit in her last conversation with Ralph Touchett. He has asked her whether or not she will return to Osmond;

'Why should there be pain? In such hours as this what have we to do with pain? That's not the deepest thing; there's something deeper . . . .'
'It passes, after all; it's passing now. But love remains. I don't know why we should suffer so much. Perhaps I shall find out. There are many things in life. You're very young.'
'I feel very old' said Isabel.
'You'll grow young again. That's how I see you . . . . I don't believe . . . that such a generous mistake as yours can hurt you for more than a little.' (630)

Such is Ralph Touchett's view. And we can be certain that it is the one we are meant to endorse.

If we compare this to the ending of *The Wings of the Dove*, where

4. Preface to *The Portrait of a Lady*.

the dying Millie Theale symbolically turns her 'face to the wall', there can be no doubt about the moral cohesion and artistic integrity of *The Portrait of a Lady*. Ernest Sandeen in an essay discussing the two novels puts the opposite point of view. He believes that James's 'willingness to subject his heroine to the same early death which belonged to his memory of Minny Temple', makes Millie 'a more profoundly tragic figure than Isabel Archer,' thereby proving James's 'greater artistic hardness' in the later work.[5] It is difficult to assent to this view in the light of Isabel's reaction to Caspar Goodwood's final appeal:

> She had wanted help, and here was help; it had come in a rushing torrent. I know not whether she believed everything he said; but she believed just then that to let him take her in his arms would be the next best thing to her dying. (643–4)

A death – a symbolic one – would have been easy, (or sentimental, if, as I suppose, Sandeen means by hard 'tough' rather than 'difficult'). But it would not have served the same artistic purpose as Milly's death does in *The Wings of the Dove*. The 'very straight path' along which Isabel perceives she must travel leads eventually back to life: and the resolution of the action, though dictated by her moral probity, is yet consonant with true spontaneity. With all her faults, Isabel represents a real American superiority, deeply felt and concretely rendered.

5. E. Sandeen, '*The Wings of the Dove* and *The Portrait of a lady*: a study of Henry James's later phase' (*PMLA*, Vol. LXIX, 1954).

4

The accumulations of civilization

Throughout his early work, James was preoccupied with the intricacies of the 'International Situation'. Towards the end of the 1880s, however, he embarked upon a long period of writing during which he confined himself to a European setting and his stories and novels came to deal more exclusively with the many-sided problems of the artist and his productions. These stories of artists reflect James's growing concern with the principles and practice of his own art, and though the works about to be discussed in the next two chapters are also directly concerned with the general themes of James's fiction they provide an excellent opportunity to notice certain criticisms of James's technique which have a bearing on those themes.

One of the defining characteristics of the nineteenth-century novel (and it was also one of the reasons for its great popularity) is that it dealt with the immediate facts of social life in a way that it was not possible for poetry to do. In the novel words are used referentially in order to create for the reader the illusion of actuality, and it is not surprising therefore, that one of the most persistent criticisms of the novel should take the form of 'Ah, but in real life things don't happen like that', couched in more or less sophisticated terminology. The criticism of fiction during the last century provides a wealth of examples of this approach, varying in subtlety from Stendhal's ambiguous plea for a novel dealing with 'what men are in a world that is', all the way down to Trollope's narrow dictum that the novel must confine itself to 'the faithful reproduction of the manners of real life'. This whole approach now appears slightly naïve in its attempts to deny the very obvious fact that the novel is more than a mere mirror of the external world of action. The attitude still persists though, and in this chapter I want to define my own dissatisfaction with certain critical estimates of *The Princess Casamassima*, and to substitute more inclusive judgements which take into account not only the author's ability to maintain a plausible illusion of real life, but also his purpose in doing so. Marianne Moore said that the job for literature is to create imaginary gardens with real toads in them.

My concern here will be primarily with the toads while at the same time acknowledging the fact that to find them one must begin by digging over the garden.

James tells us in the 1908 Preface written twenty years after the novel itself that for the hero of *The Princess Casamassima* he wanted the image of '. . . some individual nature or fine mind, some small obscure creature . . . capable of profiting by all the civilization, all the accumulations to which they testify, yet condemned to see things only from outside – in mere quickened consideration, mere wist-fulness and envy and despair.' Hyacinth Robinson certainly fulfils these specifications. He is born the illegitimate son of an English peer and a French sempstress, and is brought up by a poor dressmaker in the London slums. With such antecedents and such an environment it is not surprising that he should be drawn into revolutionary politics and come quickly into contact with anarchists like Paul Muniment, and later, the Princess Casamassima. Through these two he is introduced into a subterranean web of international intrigue, and in his enthusiasm for the revolutionary cause offers to sacrifice his life in an act of violence whenever he is called upon to do so. His offer is accepted by Hoffendahl, the mysterious leader, and he settles down to prepare himself for his task. During the period of waiting, though, Hyacinth, while still determined to do what he can for the cause, becomes disillusioned by the whole idea of revolutio-nary anarchism, and more particularly by the dubious motives of his fellow anarchists. Consequently he passes his days tortured by doubts as to the rightness of his proposed course of action, and when eventually he is commanded to assassinate the Duke, the conflict in his mind becomes unbearably acute with the result that he uses his revolver to end his own life. This then, together with the para-phernalia of the London slums and the English country house, is James's garden and no one I imagine would deny that it is all too obviously an imaginary one. On the other hand to criticize him for this unreality at the level of plot and action doesn't take one very far in understanding James's art. The following example of such criticism with its realistic premise adds nothing to our understanding of the book:

> This unfortunate but remarkably organized youth . . . is conscious of nothing but the Paradise of which he has been dispossessed . . . . In real life the last thing that would have occurred to a young man in Hyacinth's position would have been to roam and wander and yearn about the gates of that lost Paradise: he would have gone to Australia, or vanished into the slums, or continued with the utmost indifference at his trade of binding books.[1]

1. Louise Bogan quotes Van Wyck Brooks in her essay 'James on a Revolutionary Theme' (*The Nation*, Vol. CXLVI, 1938).

In the face of this one can only say that *The Princess Casamassima* is not 'real life', and that the values which James examines quite obviously preclude the presentation of Hyacinth as an Australian immigrant or an indifferent book-binder. Before going on to see what these values are, let us turn to another kind of criticism which seeks to defend the literary accuracy of *The Princess Casamassima* against such attacks as that made by Van Wyck Brooks. Lionel Trilling, after giving a short history of anarchism in the nineteenth century, goes on to say that he finds the novel extremely accurate, even in its detail, and that it is a '. . . brilliantly precise representation of social actuality'. He gives examples from the past hundred years to show that there is not '. . . a political event of *The Princess Casamassima*, not a detail of oath, or mystery or danger, which is not confirmed by multitudinous records.'[2] Again, Trilling may be right. But whether he is or not his defence is as irrelevant as the criticism which provoked it. James himself tells us that he was not concerned with producing a well authenticated record of the times:

> What it all came back to was doubt, something like this wisdom – that if you haven't, for fiction, the root of the matter in you, haven't the sense of life and penetrating imagination, you are a fool in the very presence of the revealed and assured: but that if you are so armed you are not really helpless, not without your resource, even before mysteries abysmal.[3]

To show that James was neither a 'fool in the presence of the revealed', nor on the other hand, a second-rate Zola, we must discover what exactly for him, the root of the matter was.

What I have called the paraphernalia of the London slums and the English country house, though not treated realistically, does help to define the contending moral and aesthetic values, both of which seem to Hyacinth quite fundamental yet also mutually exclusive, and which lead eventually to his suicide. His uncomplicated existence as a social reformer comes to an end when he is invited by the Princess to stay at her country house. It is his first real contact with the 'accumulations of civilization', and his reaction is not what one would have expected:

> There was something in the way the grey walls rose from the green lawns that brought tears to his eyes; the spectacle of long duration unassociated with some sordid infirmity of poverty was new to him; he had lived with people among whom old age meant, for the most part, a grudged and degraded survival. In the majestic preservation of Medley there was a kind of serenity of success, and accumulation of dignity and honour. (II, 6–7)

2. *The Liberal Imagination* (New York, 1950).
3. Preface to *The Princess Casamassima*.

In this way, then, the complication is brought about. At the height of his revolutionary ardour, when his hatred of social injustice is at its most searing, he is suddenly made aware of the beauty of the world: a beauty which is dependent on the very injustices he is pledged to eliminate. Ultimately, what this problem comes down to is a conflict of views about the nature of civilization itself. There can be no doubt that James had great sympathy with the advocates of social reform; it is apparent in the Princess's passionate denunciation of the English upper classes, which is taken almost exactly as it stands from one of James's letters to Charles Eliot Norton:

> The condition of that body seems to me to be in many ways very much the same rotten and collapsible one as that of the French aristocracy before the revolution – minus cleverness and conversation; or perhaps it's more like the heavy, congested and depraved Roman world upon which the barbarians came down. In England the Huns and Vandals will have to come up – from the black depths of the (in the people) enormous misery, though I don't think the Attila is quite yet found. (I, 125)

But balancing this moral fervour is Hyacinth's and James's concern with the preservation of the finer products of our civilization, and Hyacinth's letter from Venice expresses the same sort of horror at the thought of what will happen to them at the hands of the Nihilists, as James himself appeared to feel at the outbreak of the First World War when he believed the end of European civilization was imminent. Here then is part of Hyacinth's long, crucial letter:

> I have found them [suffering and toil] everywhere, but haven't minded them. Excuse the cynical profession. What has struck me is the great achievements of which man has been capable in spite of them – the splendid accumulations of the happier few, to which, doubtless, the miserable many have also in their degree contributed. The face of Europe appears to be covered with them, and they have had much the greater part of my attention. They seem to me inestimably precious and beautiful, and I have become conscious, more than ever before, of how little I understand what, in the great rectification, you and Poupin propose to do with them. Dear Princess, there are things which I shall be sorry to see you touch, even you with your hands divine; and – shall I tell you *le fond de ma pensée*, as you used to say? – I feel myself capable of fighting for them. You can't call me a traitor for you know the obligation I recognize. The monuments and treasures of art, the great palaces and properties, the conquests of learning and taste, the general fabric of civilization as we know it, based, if you will, upon all the despotisms, the cruelties, the exclusions, the monopolies and rapacities of the past, but thanks to which all the same, the world is less impracticable and life more tolerable – our friend Hoffendahl seems to me to hold them too cheap and to wish to substitute for them something in which I can't somehow believe as I do in things with which the aspirations and the tears of generations have been mixed. You know how extraordinary I think our Hoffendahl (to speak

only of him); but if there is one thing that is more clear about him than another it is that he wouldn't have the least feeling for this incomparable, abominable old Venice. He would cut up the ceilings of the Veronese into strips, so that everyone might have a little piece. I don't want everyone to have a little piece of anything, and I have a great horror of that kind of invidious jealousy which is at the bottom of the idea of the re-distribution . . .. I don't know what it comes from, but during the last three months there has crept over me a deep mistrust of that same grudging attitude – the intolerance of positions and fortunes that are higher and brighter than one's own; a fear moreover, that I may, in the past, have been actuated by such motives, and the devout hope that if I am to pass away while I am yet young it may not be with that odious stain upon my soul. (II, 130–1]

It might be argued that to cut up the ceilings of the Veronese into strips is a programme that could only be envisaged by Nihilists and that James's problem concerning the rival claims of art and moral action concerns an imaginary toad in an imaginary garden. But the evidence from 'real life' indicates that this is not really the case. Lenin, for one, felt the problem as an acute one but offered an alternative solution. After listening to a Beethoven sonata, he is quoted as saying: 'I'll always think with pride . . . what marvellous things human beings can do. But I can't listen to music too often. It affects your nerves, makes you want to say nice things and stroke the heads of people who could create such beauty while living in this vile hell. And now, you mustn't stroke anyone's head – you might get your hand bitten off.'[4]

The Princess is in this one respect like Lenin. She too is afraid that she might get her hand bitten off if she allows private emotions to divert her from public ends. So afraid is she of this that she repudiates all her wealth and treasures (except for one or two bibelots, James tells us with characteristic irony). She even repudiates Hyacinth, whose complex awareness of the values at stake makes her simple moralism appear altogether ridiculous; and he, in an attempt to resolve his doubts, commits suicide.

This solution, while satisfying the demands of a particular situation, doesn't help at all in clarifying James's own idea of the nature of an ideal culture. Trilling, in his Introduction to *The Princess Casamassima* maintains that:

> It is a novel which has at its very centre the assumption that Europe has reached the full of its ripeness and is passing over into rottenness, that the peculiarly beautiful light it gives forth is in part the reflection of a glorious past and in part the phosphorescence of a present decay, that it may meet its end by violence and that this is not wholly unjust, although never before has the old sinful Continent made so proud and pathetic assault upon our affections.

4. Quoted by Edmund Wilson in *The Triple Thinkers* (London, 1938).

Here again the issue is over-simplified. The assault which Europe makes is not intended to be merely upon our affections but upon everything in us that responds to what is beautiful – to the 'accumulations of civilization'; for the 'rottenness' that Trilling writes about was not for James a new discovery but was and always had been a corollary of European civilization necessitating in the earlier 'European' novels the heroes' or heroines' retreat from that civilization, or in the case Roderick Hudson his defeat by it. What distinguishes *The Princess Casamassima* is Hyacinth's and James's inability to make a choice between political or moral action on the one hand, and art on the other. James, of course, in actual fact, had made the choice years before when he had first decided to become a novelist and his inability only consists in his failure to provide any entirely satisfactory justification for the choice. He was, though, through the medium of his novels working his way towards such an end and he seemed to have achieved it in the stories he wrote during the 1890s. Before discussing these it might be illuminating to examine the reactions of another novelist, E. M. Forster, when confronted with an almost identical situation, for Forster's choice, and the arguments he uses to justify it, help to clarify the nature of the issue and to demonstrate its urgent appeal.

Howard's End even more than *The Princess Casamassima* has been a target for the criticism of the social realists. Forster has been accused of a fundamental irresponsibility, a lack of seriousness, and of doctoring the issue. The novel has been made the occasion for an attack on Forster's 'liberal idealism', and also for a more general attack on the 'leisured bourgeois parasites' depicted in his novels. All these charges seem to have been made by critics who themselves are determined to evade the issue by adhering to a rigid and inadequate conception of reality. Even if, after reading *Howard's End*, we wish to say that Forster's ideal of the real is inadequate, at least it must be admitted that it is more inclusive than that held by those who summarily dismiss the problem he presents by calling it non-existent.

The dramatic action of the novel develops out of the efforts of two sisters to achieve a way of life that is consonant with the facts of modern capitalist society. They are cultured, moderately rich, and quite out of touch with what they call the 'outer life'. Helen Schlegel, who is less sensitive, and more idealistic than her siter, chooses the wrong path. She is like the Princess in *The Princess Casamassima;* following an impulse that is neither fully understood, nor fully controlled, she deliberately cultivates and accidentally destroys a poor insurance clerk, Leonard Bast. Forster's portrait of Bast has often been criticized, not least by those who call *Howard's End* a justification of economic privilege. On the contrary, the portrayal of

Leonard Bast is a minor triumph. He is, we are told, 'one of those who have lost the life of the body and failed to reach the life of the spirit.' Forster with characteristic moral realism refuses to sentimentalize him:

> The boy, Leonard Bast, stood at the extreme verge of gentility. He was not in the abyss, but he could see it, and at times people who he knew had dropped in, and counted no more. He knew that he was poor and would admit it: he would have died rather than confess any inferiority to the rich. This may be splendid of him. But he was inferior to most rich people, there is not the least doubt of it . . . . His mind and his body alike had been underfed because he was poor.

This passage in particular has been severely criticized on the grounds that Leonard Bast is not the result of authentic, disinterested observation: that he is a lay figure put in to bolster the liberal philosophy which inspires the book. Forster's theme, we are told, is not likely to find any response in the mind of the genuine champion of the under-privileged masses, for the depth of his concern with the suffering of the dispossessed may be judged from the fact that it is Henry Wilcox (the rich capitalist) with whom Margaret Schlegel 'connects'. This surely is to treat literature as distilled sociology, and Forster, like James, is not so much concerned with solving sociological problems as in exploring the moral impulses that manifest themselves in all human relationships and institutions. His public theme in *Howard's End* is similar to James's in *The Princess Casamassima:* the dependence of culture and the 'accumulations of civilization' on the commercial enterprise and goodwill of a few entrepreneurs, and the consequences for this culture of a changing society. Forster develops the inherent conflict in this situation not by having a revolutionary group pledge themselves to destroy the 'treasures of art', but merely by showing how the present-day Wilcoxes are, for a variety of reasons, indifferent to the continuance of art. He developed this theme and provided a solution to the problem in an essay written in 1940 called *Does Culture Matter?*;

> It is impossible to be fair minded when one has faith – religious creeds have shown this – and I have so much faith in cultural stuff that I believe it must mean something to other people, and anyhow want it left lying about . . . .. Our problem, as I see it, is this: is what we have got worth passing on? What we have got is (roughly speaking) a little knowledge about books, pictures, tunes, and a little skill in their interpretation. Seated beside our gas-fires, and beneath our electric bulbs, we inherit a tradition which has lasted for about three thousand years. The tradition was partly popular but mainly dependent upon aristocratic patronage. In the past culture has been paid for by the ruling classes; they often did not know why they paid, but they paid, much as they went to church; it was the

proper thing to do, it was a form of social snobbery, and so the artist
sneaked a meal, the author got a sinecure, and the work of creation went
on. Today, people are coming to the top, who are in some ways, more
clearsighted and honest than the ruling classes of the past, and they refuse
to pay for what they don't want; judging by the noises through the floor,
our neighbour in the flat above doesn't want books, pictures, tunes,
runes, anyhow doesn't want the sorts which we recommend. Ought we to
bother him? When he is hurrying to lead his own life, ought we to get in
his way like a maiden aunt, our arms, as it were, full of parcels, and say to
him, 'I was given these specially to hand on to you . . . Sophocles,
Velasquez, Henry James . . . I am afraid they are a little heavy, but you'll
get to love them in time, and if you don't take them off my hands, I don't
know who will . . . . Please . . . please . . . they're really important,
they're culture.'[5]

Forster concludes that it is our job to spread culture 'not because we
love our fellow men, but because certain things seem to us unique
and priceless, and, as it were, push us out into the world on their
service.'

He also attempts to provide a solution in *Howard's End*. Margaret
Schlegel is fully aware of the antagonistic principles which, incapable
of resolution in Hyacinth Robinson's mind, are responsible for his
suicide. Her avowed mission, however, is to achieve a compromise,
which is symbolically effected when she marries Henry Wilcox.
'Only connect! that was the whole of her sermon. Only connect the
prose and the passion, and both will be exalted, and human love will
be seen at its height.' The connection is made, but the result is an
uneasy compromise – an unsatisfactory protest against what Forster
calls 'the inner darkness in high places that comes with a commercial
age.'

James's protest was unsatisfactory too, and he himself may have
felt this, for in 1890, four years after the publication of *The Princess
Casamassima*, he again turned to the problem of the incompatibility
of the artistic life with that of the politician. As a result he produced
what was to have been his last long novel, *The Tragic Muse*. A similar
conflict is analysed in the stories he wrote throught the 1890s.

5. *Two Cheers for Democracy* (London, 1951).

5

Our passion is our task

One of the obvious disadvantages of living in the 'global village' created by mass-media is the forced diminution and eventual disappearance of that area in which the individual consciousness can develop and expand. At such a time it is not surprising that we should have to be reminded in newspaper articles written by famous authors that literature has to do with living. What is surprising is that in the course of such an article Lionel Trilling can say:

> Think for instance, of some of the minor – good but not momentous – stories of Henry James; how he could just go on, endlessly, spinning these webs of narrative about individuals. I think he was perfectly justified in doing so, but I couldn't do it myself. It would be a pleasure, even a luxury; but when I settle down to think over possible plots for an interesting novel, I feel the need to choose one that has a direct bearing on public events.[1]

I imagine that the stories about to be discussed fall into Trilling's category of 'good, but not momentous'. They are certainly stories about individuals in a way that Trilling's own novel *The Middle of the Journey* isn't, and the characters in them do not display any explicit awareness of the 'major battles' of the time. But this is just what marks James off as a creative genius and gives his work that 'solidity of specification' often lacking in Trilling's. James's ability to infer the political macrocosm from the personal microcosm is testified to by Trilling himself elsewhere as a matter of fact.[2] And even when James did tackle head-on the 'grosser movements of society and civilization' in *The Bostonians* and *The Princess Casamassima*, it was largely in an effort to capture a public that had hitherto failed him, as was his excursion into playwriting some years later. His inability to win a wide audience by these means turned him back to spinning 'webs of narrative about individuals', but his continued preoccupation with the problem was now incorporated into his fiction as a theme.

1. 'Literature and Life', *The Observer* (London, September 1957).
2. *The Opposing Self* (London, 1955).

The stories in question, 'The Lesson of the Master', 'The Death of the Lion', 'The Next Time', 'The Author of Beltraffio' and one or two others, are all stories about the artist's relation to society, and they show James still singlemindedly struggling with the problems of art and moral action at a time when most of his contemporaries were taking aestheticism to its logical extremes. How he resolves his problem is no more important than how the problems came to present themselves, and the answer to this question involves not only the history of James's development as an artist but also the history of our culture. Certain facts connected with that history have an obvious relevance, providing the frame of reference without which it is impossible even to see James, let alone criticize him.

It is customary to account for many modern phenomena – social, artistic, economic, religious or political – in terms of the Industrial Revolution. Not only Marxists do this; we have all been doing it for so long that historians often find it necesary to apologize for taking us over the familiar ground yet again. Our reflexes are so well conditioned that we have long since ceased to take it seriously and ask pertinent questions about it. We know, for example, that the power loom was invented in 1784, but what, we might legitimately ask, had this to do with the monstrosities displayed at the Great Exhibition of 1851? And what had Victorian morality to do with the fact that private patronage of the arts was almost non-existent by 1800? Questions like these, involving the inter-relatedness of different fields of activity, are never easy to answer; but just because they lead the mind to considerations of the relationship of ethics to experimental science, or economics to inductive philosophy, they are well worth asking. For the literary critic, perhaps the most important single strand in the pattern of English history is the succession – as patrons of the arts – of the Church, the Court, the nobility, the political parties, the bourgeoisie and the State.

Although the country-house civilization known to Ben Jonson and his contemporaries had been superseded by the time of the Restoration, private patronage of the arts, which was a mark of that culture, continued well into the eighteenth century. It was supplemented, though, by political subvention, necessitated by the close division of power between the Whigs and Tories under William III and Anne. Neither party could afford to forego the use of propaganda, and consequently they employed the services of men like Addison, Steele, and Swift, who took the opportunity both to enrich themselves and to raise the prestige of the artist. Addison, for example, not only became a Secretary of State with a pension of sixteen hundred pounds but also managed to marry a Countess. But the over-whelming victory of Walpole in 1721 put an end to political patronage and until the end of the century most writers led a fairly precarious existence, either as literary hacks, or in the service of a private patron. The complaints against patronage during this period on the grounds that it was a humiliating relationship, form an interesting commentary on the changing social patterns in general. The emergence of the publisher in the last years of the eighteenth century coincided with the liberation of middle-class taste and the rise to power of the bourgeoisie. The production of books, for a public unknown to the author, is what one might expect in an impersonal, capitalist economy, and although it assured the material independence of the writer, it must also share in the responsibility for his spiritual isolation and for the rise of Romanticism, culminating in the aestheticism of the 1890s. In England and France, reaction against the bourgeois way of life was carried to extremes by Rimbaud, Verlaine, Tristan Corbière, Baudelaire, Whistler, Wilde and Beardsley, whose dandyism and bohemianism as a protest against the prevalent philistinism were carried over from their art into their lives.

It is against this background that James's stories of artists came to be written, and indeed several of them made their first appearance in *The Yellow Book*. It is true that he hated the 'horrid aspect' of the magazine, and professed only to contribute for the sake of money; but in spite of the difference in quality and tone between his stories and those of his fellow contributors they do not seem entirely out of place there. *The Death of the Lion* is an angry outburst against the dullness of contemporary society whose only use for the great artist is for him to 'irrigate their social flowerbeds'. When Neil Paraday is taken up by the public his young admirer has a vision of what this is going to mean:

> The big blundering newspapers had discovered him, and now he was proclaimed and anointed and crowned. His place was assigned to him as publicly as if a fat usher with a wand had pointed to the topmost chair; he was to pass up and still up, higher and higher, between the watching faces and the envious sounds – away up to the dais and the throne. The article was 'epoch-making', a landmark in his life: he had taken rank at a bound, waked up a national glory. A national glory was needed, and it was an immense convenience he was there . . .. When Neil Paraday should come out of the house he would come out a contemporary. That was what had happened: the poor man was to be squeezed into his horrible age. I felt as if he had been overtaken on the crest of a hill and brought back to the city. A little more and he would have dipped down the short cut to posterity and escaped. (*The Lesson of the Master and Other Stories*, 86)

Eventually the Philistine, Mrs Wimbush-Weeks, is responsible for his death and is instrumental in losing the manuscript of his greatest novel, having first assured herself 'of a great reputation for patronage of intellectual and other merits' by 'lending Paraday the most beautiful of her numerous homes to die in.'

This is James at his most savage and bitter, declaiming like Pope in the *Epistle to Burlington*, against the 'horrible age'. Unlike Pope though, he does not in these stories specify the conditions for a better society. On the contrary, in the Preface to 'The Lesson of the Master' he appears to have despaired of doing this and is content 'in the midst of all the stupidity and vulgarity' to create the fine sensibility capable of reaction against these things. F. R. Leavis suggested that had James been a member of the Sidgwick circle he might have written differently; but I doubt it. No matter what the quality of life described (think of the Wentworths in *The Europeans*) it is always opposed to art. The only chance for the artist, and in fact it is really no chance at all, is to have a dual self like Clare Vawdrey in 'The Private Life,' who 'when the world was old and stupid . . . would have been a fool to come out of his study, when he could gossip and dine by deputy', This quotation admirably summarizes James's attitude in all the stories. He cannot bring himself to talk of life without prefixing the adjectives 'clumsy', 'brutal', or 'vulgar'. He seems to believe, like Thomas Mann's *bourgeois manqué* Tonio Kröger, that

> . . . feeling, warm heartfelt feeling, is always banal and futile; only the imitations and icy ecstasies of the artist's corrupted nervous system are artistic. The artist must be unhuman, extra human; he must stand in a queer aloof relationship to our humanity.

In fact, *Tonio Kröger* exactly complements James's fine story *The Lesson of the Master*. Tonio Kröger is an 'artist with a bad conscience', 'a bourgeois who strayed off into art, a Bohemian who feels nostalgic yearning for respectability'. He is an artist who is driven to seek the 'icy ecstasies', but whose deepest and most secret love belongs to the ideal Nietzschean type, 'the blonde and blue-eyed, the fair and living'. Like James, Mann knows that in a sense one must die to life in order to be a creator, but it is a death, or in his own imagery, a disease which he bitterly resents. In *Tonio Kröger*, as in *Death in Venice* and *Buddenbrooks*, art is synonymous with moral decay, whereas in 'The Lesson of the Master' James maintains that the artist can best preserve his integrity by renouncing completely the claims of life.

Henry St George, a novelist of great talent, has deliberately sold out, as it were, to 'the idols of the market – money and luxury and the world; placing one's children and dressing one's wife' and consequently he has got everything except 'the great thing':

> 'The sense of having done the best – the sense which is the real life of the artist and the absence of which is his death, of having drawn from his intellectual instrument the finest music that nature had hidden in it, of

having played it as it should be played. He either does that or he doesn't – and if he doesn't he isn't worth speaking of. Therefore, precisely, those who really know don't speak of him. He may still hear a great chatter, but what he hears most is the incorruptible silence of Fame.' (61)

In a series of conversations with a young novelist, Paul Overt, St George implores him to leave the woman he loves and dedicate himself to art. James allows Overt to state the case for life in the strongest possible terms, but he knows as does St George, that it is the icy ecstasies that matter. Here is part of their conversation:

'You've had the full rich masculine human general life, with all the responsibilities and duties and burdens and sorrows and joys – all the domestic and social initiations and complications. They must be immensely suggestive, immensely amusing,' Paul anxiously submitted.

'Amusing?'

'For a strong man – yes.'

'They've given me subjects without number, if that's what you mean: but they've taken away at the same time the power to use them. I've touched a thousand things, but which one of them have I turned into gold? The artist has to do only with that – he knows nothing of any baser metal. I've led the life of the world, my wife and my progeny; the clumsy conventional expensive materialized vulgarized brutalized life of London. We've got everything handsome, even a carriage – we're perfect capital Philistines and prosperous hospitable eminent people. But my dear fellow, don't try to stultify yourself and pretend you don't know what we *haven't* got. It's bigger than all the rest.' (63)

Overt agrees but what he really wants is a life in which the 'passion – ours, is really intense', and to this end he renounces his suit and goes abroad for two years to write a novel. On his return he finds St George, whose wife has in the meantime died, on the point of marrying the girl he himself gave up. At first he is bitterly disillusioned, sensing that he has been tricked, but as time passes and St George continues to publish nothing, and as his own work increases in stature, he perceives that 'the Master was essentially right and that Nature had dedicated him to intellectual, not personal passion.' One cannot help but notice the strong autobiographical element in this story, and also in one which is antithetical to it, 'The Next Time.' This concerns the efforts of a great but obscure novelist, Ray Linbert, to write a popular success. However, he is doomed to preserve his artistic integrity, even against his own will. Like James, when he wrote occasional pieces for American magazines, he just couldn't write badly enough to be popular.

Similarly in *'The Tragic Muse,'* James appears to be dramatizing the conflict which he himself felt so keenly, and which he argued about so fiercely in his letters to William. He had always had, he says, 'some dramatic picture of the "artist-life" and of the difficult terms on which it is at the best secured and enjoyed, the general questions of its having to be not altogether easily paid for. To "do something about art" – art, that is, as a human complication and a social stumbling-block must have been for me early a good deal of mixed intention, a conflict between art and the "world" striking me thus betimes as one of the half-dozen great primary motives'.[3] As he so often found, his chief difficulty lay in presenting the conflict in terms which would do justice to the artist's renunciation of the 'great obvious, great moral or functional or useful character'. James knew from his experience what sacrifices were required to enable the artist to eat the cake of the 'very rarest privilege, the most luscious baked in the oven of the gods'; but he also knew that all the world sees of the artist's triumph is the 'back he turns to us as he bends over his work', and that to the majority his sacrifice must seem like 'a surrender for absolutely nothing'. To obviate this reaction on the part of the reader, James, who had, as he reminds us in the Preface, 'gained a more and more intimate view of the nature of art', uses all his knowledge and craft to persuade us of the essential rightness of Nick Dormer's choice. To do so, not only has he to compare Nick's position with the one he might have attained to in public life, but also he has to rescue the idea of the artistic life from the popular conception of it: from a conviction that 'the aesthetic – a horrible insidious foreign disease – is eating the healthy core of English life (dear old English life).'

James approaches this task with complete seriousness and honesty, and allows Nick Dormer the same doubts and misgiving which he himself had experienced. One passage in particular complements that in *A Small Boy and Others* in which James describes a visit to the *Galerie d'Apollon*. Critics have made much of this passage,[4] finding in it clues to almost everything in James's subsequent life and work, but what stands out principally in his description of the episode is the sense of glory which came to him in the great gallery; a glory which meant many things at once, 'not only beauty and art and supreme design, but history and fame and power, the world in fine raised to the richest and noblest expression.' Similarly, Nick Dormer, visiting the National Gallery realizes that politics need not be only the love of 'hollow, idiotic words', and that the claims of the 'world' may indeed be more imperative than those of art:

> What had happened to him, as he passed on this occasion from Titian to Rubens, and from Gainsborough to Rembrandt, was that he found

3. Preface to *The Tragic Muse*.
4. Especially Leon Edel in *Henry James: the Untried Years* 1843–1870 (London, 1953).

himself calling the whole art literally into question. What was it after all, at the best, and why had people given it so high a place? Its weakness, its narrowness appeared to him; tacitly blaspheming he looked at several world-famous performances with a lustreless eye . . . . The force that produced them was not one of the greatest forces in human affairs: their place was inferior and their connection with the life of man casual and slight. They represented so inadequately the idea, and it was the idea that won the race, that in the long run came in first. He had incontestably been in much closer relation to the idea a few months before than he was today: it made up a great deal for the bad side of politics that they were after all a clumsy system for applying and propagating the idea. (487–8)

This episode comes at a crisis in Nick's life, analogous to that described in Hyacinth Robinson's letter from Venice. With the help of his friend and mentor Gabriel Nash, however, he comes eventually to the decision that 'nothing on earth would induce him to turn back again: not even if this twilight of the soul should last for the rest of his days.' Nash is not so sure though, and he prophesies that Julia Dallow, Nick's former fiancée, and his main tie with the world of politics, will eventually undermine his determination and draw him back into the world.[5] Gabriel Nash's description of that world is reminiscent of James's own in 'The Death of the Lion':

'She'll get you down to one of the country houses, and it will all go off charmingly – with sketching in the morning, on days you can't hunt, and anything you like in the afternoon, and fifteen courses in the evening . . .. You'll go about with her and all her friends, all the bishops and ambassadors, and you'll eat your cake and have it, and everyone, beginning with your wife, will forget there's anything queer about you, and everything will be for the best in the best of worlds.' (592)

Whether Nash's prophecy will be fulfilled is not made clear in the novel, though it is true that Nick does accept an invitation from Julia, and does sketch the company, growing rather red, we are told, when he thinks of Gabriel Nash. Nor does it much matter whether or not Nick Dormer actually succumbs to the temptations held out to him by the world. James had succeeded in doing what he set out to do: in showing the integrity and single-minded devotion involved in the 'artist-life'.

The problems which beset the artist concerning his relation to society and to life in general provide a constant stimulus, and Eliot, Lawrence, Kafka and Mann all, whether directly or indirectly, make it a subject of their art. D. H. Lawrence, in his essay on Galsworthy, defines what he calls 'the collapse from the psychology of the free

5. L. H. Powers argues, ingeniously, that despite these hints to the contrary, James works his theme out to its logical conclusion – 'the persistent triumph of art'. 'James's *The Tragic Muse* — Ave Atque Vale.' (*PMLA*, Vol. LXXIII, 1958).

human individual into the psychology of the social being', and in doing so admirably sums up the predicament of all James's artists:

> It seems to me that when the human being becomes too much divided between his subjective and objective consciousness, at last somethings splits in him and he becomes a social being.

James was very well aware of the dangers involved in becoming such a 'social being', and he deals with some of these in the novels which follow *The Tragic Muse*.

6

The imagination of disaster

James once wrote of philosophy: 'I imagine that almost any *practicant* artist is necessarily out of almost any discussion of these mysteries and subtleties. At any rate they only make me cuddle closer to my little vulgar, personal special empirical industry. *Tout est là.*'[1] It pays to keep this in mind when reading *The Spoils of Poynton,* for it is only too easy to see the book as an elaborate web of ethical speculation woven for the author's pleasure out of an abstract academic terminology and owing nothing to the discoverable facts of human experience – a study in the psychology of ethical absolutism as one critic calls it.[2] James has achieved a rigid economy which effectively eliminates all that for most people means life – the 'fringes' that, says Edith Wharton 'we trail after us through life, and which provide the novelist with his material, or the 'hum of implication' that accompanies the interaction of human lives according to Lionel Trilling. These are absent in *The Spoils of Poynton,* displaced by the all but disembodied sensibility 'discriminating and selecting from the surrounding tangle of inclusion and confusion which is life.' Confronted with this the critic may complain that there is no warrant in life for so fine a moral sensibility as that of Fleda Vetch. To him James has no hesitation in rejoining: 'So much the worse for life.' This is just the point he wishes to make – that the facts of human experience are, generally speaking, inadequate for the novelist's purpose. He must create his imaginative ideal which is, of course, if only by implication, also a criticism of the actual.

Within *The Spoils of Poynton* criticism operates at different levels of seriousness as aesthetic and moral deficiencies are revealed first by the more, and gradually by the less limited sensibilities of the characters. The way in which this is achieved is itself a minor triumph of fictional organization. But it is with the force and relative inclusiveness of these criticisms that we are mainly concerned, and this depends on the view we take of the main characters, their

1. Letter to Henry B. Brewster published in *Botteghe Oscure*, No. 10. 1957.
2. P. F. Quinn, 'Morals and Motives in *The Spoils of Poynton*' (*The Sewanee Review*, Vol. LXII, 1954).

reactions to each other, and to Poynton and 'the things'. The 'felt beauty and value' of the things, constitutes James says, 'the citadel of the interest', and projects a sharp light on 'that most modern of our current passions, the fierce appetite for the upholsterers' and joiners' and glaziers' work, the chairs and tables, the cabinets and presses, the material odds and ends of the more labouring ages.'[3]

Mrs Gereth's attitude to them is quite unambiguous. Despite her passion for them – 'they were our religion, they were our life, they were us' – she remains disinterested and free from greed. 'It was absolutely unselfish. She cared nothing for mere possession. She thought solely and incorruptibly of what was best for the things.' Everything in her is subordinated to this passion for the beautiful. After a lifetime devoted to art she had come to have 'no perception of anybody's nature – had only one question about persons: were they clever or stupid.' To be clever meant to know the marks. 'Fleda knew them by direct inspiration, and the warm recognition of this had been her friends' tribute to her character.' The difference between them is that although 'almost as much as Mrs Gereth, her taste was her life – her life was somehow the larger for it.' The high lucidity James endows her with enables her to see that the kind of experience cherished by Mrs Gereth was 'so clearly so broken a reed, so fallible a source of peace.' Fleda transcends her taste, has 'hours of sombre hope she might never see anything good again', and eventually 'becomes rather fine, does something, distinguishes herself.' The story is set in motion by the fact that Mrs Gereth is obliged to leave Poynton which, by the terms of her husband's will, goes to their son Owen, a dull, amiable and malleable individual who is engaged to be married to Mona Brigstock. Mona, an important character, but relatively simple and therefore not intrinsically interesting to James is

> . . . all will, without the smallest leak of force into taste or tenderness or vision, into any sense of shades or relations or proportions. She loses no minute in that perception of incongruities in which half Fleda's passion is wasted and misled, and into which Mrs Gereth, to her practical loss, that is by the fatal grace of a sense of comedy, occasionally and disinterestedly strays. Everyone, everything, in the story is accordingly sterile *but* the so thriftily constucted Mona, able at any moment to bear he whole of her dead weight at once on any given inch of a resisting surface.[4]

In an effort to prevent her son's marriage, Mrs Gereth suddenly leaves Poynton taking with her most of the things. It is apparent that Mona is interested only in acquiring the 'spoils', and for some time it looks as though Mrs Gereth's plan will be successful, for the

3. Preface to *The Spoils of Poynton*.
4. *Ibid.*

wedding is indefinitely postponed and Fleda (who is aware of the plan) and Owen find themselves falling in love. However, it is at this point that Fleda's moral scruples come so strongly into play. She will not take any action to jeopardize the engagement, considering it an irrevocable and final commitment. 'Pledges so deep, so sacred. How could Fleda doubt they had been tremendous when she knew so well what any pledge of her own would be.' She insists that Owen should take no action and together they wait for Mona to break the engagement. Mrs Gereth, whose personality excludes her from an understanding of such niceties of behaviour, returns the things, believing that she has accomplished her ends. However, this move only serves to attract Mona once again and the outcome is that it is she and not Fleda who finally marries Owen. Reserving his ultimate irony for the last page, James there shows how futile the pursuit was by having Poynton gutted by fire during its owner's absence abroad.

So much then for what is 'given', simply in the exposition of plot and character delineation. If it is true that the principal interest of the novel lies in the force of the criticisms made by or exemplified by the actions of the principal characters then it is here that we must look for James's experience of a total view of the world. It would appear that in these novels of the middle period the moral consciousness resumes some of the importance it had in *Portrait of a Lady* and *The Europeans*. Maisie, Nanda and Fleda typify the prized purity and innocence of James's early American heroines and there is a growing sense of the inadequacy of mere aesthetic value indiscriminately applied. Whilst there is no doubting James's admiration for Mrs Gereth, it is nevertheless qualified by a sharp sense of her complete lack of moral scruple. They are all – Mrs Gereth, Fleda and James in himself – horrified by Waterbath, the Brigstock's home:

> It was an ugliness fundamental and systematic, the result of the abnormal nature of the Brigstocks, from whose composition the principle of taste had been extravagantly omitted. In the arrangement of the home some other principle, remarkably active, but uncanny and obscure, had operated instead, with consequences depressing to behold, consequences that took the form of a universal futility. The house was bad in all conscience, but it might have passed if they had only let it alone. This saving mercy was beyond them; they had smothered it with trumpery ornament and scrapbook art, with strange excrescences and bunchy draperies, with gimcracks that might have been keepsakes for maidservants and nondescript conveniences that might have been prizes for the blind. They had gone wildly astray over carpets and curtains; they had an infallible instinct for gross deviation and were so cruelly doom-ridden that it rendered them almost tragic. (6)

Although Mrs Gereth's horror is justified here James is careful to insist that her 'scruples were all on one side and her ruling passion had in a manner despoiled her of her humanity'. To reinforce his criticism of her he introduces Fleda's father whose collection of shabby objects parodies that of Mrs Gereth: 'old brandy flasks and match-boxes, old calendars and hand-books intermixed with an assortment of penwipers and ash-trays, a harvest gathered from penny bazaars.' This, though, is not a very satisfactory criticism. It presents too easy a solution to a problem essentially complex. Juxtaposed, Mrs Gereth and Fleda's father make each other seem ridiculous with their unshakeable faith in mutually exclusive passions, but the implied contrast between their aesthetic sensibilities and Fleda's moral sense does not hold at all. Moral laws are just as relative – or fallible – as aesthetic ones. Similarly with the fire at Poynton, it poses the futility of the passion for beauty all right, but the implied contrast with the passion for good, doesn't hold at all. Unsatisfactory as James's criticism seems, there can be no doubt that this interpretation is correct. At any rate it is difficult to accept the alternative interpretation as put forward by Patrick Quinn:

> 'Mr Vetch's sublime faith in the excellence of his aesthetic judgement is patently absurd. Later on Fleda will act on a quite similar faith in the finality of her ethical judgement. Father and daughter are both absolutists, in different ways both may be blind. In a few lines given to Mr Vetch, we have a reflector, a marker, by which the book as a whole may be better seen.

There is ample evidence that James didn't intend the reader to make this interpretation, as Mr Quinn himself says in another part of his essay. Must we then, suppose that James is as blind as his characters?

Having very easily disposed of Mona's vulgar greed and Owen's weakness, and with more difficulty of Mrs Gereth, who although of a remarkably fine taste is the reverse of a free spirit, James feels free to enlarge on Fleda's virtues, and it is with his own view of Fleda that criticism must eventually come to terms. There is no doubt at all that for James Fleda represents some kind of an ideal. It is enough for him to say that 'she *does* something', and as the editors of James's Notebooks say 'he had a full awareness of what he was trying for. He wanted to present Fleda as the quintessence of the "free spirit".' But criticism cannot end there. Is James's idea of the free spirit satisfactory? Most people would say 'No'. Even if we agree that she has a 'certain high lucidity' and a wonderful understanding of the situation, the action she takes, and the action she fails to take appear as an abuse of her freedom. Many critics have pointed out that even in those books which are usually called the 'English Novels', the international situation is never very far below the surface, and in *The Spoils of Poynton* James has obviously once again created his ideal of

American innocence. What he doesn't seem capable of appreciating is the terrible self-destructive power that is wielded by these innocents. Fleda by her refusal to lend herself, not to expediency which would be base but to a utilitarian ethic even, despoils herself of humanity just as much as Mrs Gereth. She retains her absolute integrity, but effectively ruins the lives of those she loves. Time after time she is brought up against the consequences of her rigid morality. Consequences which are repugnant even to herself, as when Owen asks her:

> 'Do you mean to tell me that I must marry the woman I hate? . . .'
> 'No, anything is better than that . . .'
> 'Then, in God's name, what must I do?'
> 'You must settle that with Mona. You mustn't break faith.' (172)

More perhaps than any of James's heroines she has a passion for renunciation and suffering. Even when she temporarily gives herself up to her feeling for Owen it is never a complete surrender:

> She poured out her tears on his breast; something prisoned and pent throbbed and gushed; something deep and sweet surged up. Yet the strongest sense of all was the momentary sense of desolation. (165)

For her, life is not only crude and vulgar, it is also a menace to be kept at a distance. Like James she has the imagination of disaster and sees life as ferocious and sinister. There is about her an excess of refinement which renders her literally repulsive. Her preoccupation with moral questions is not in the interest of life but rather a rationalization of her impulse to self-destruction.

One of the confusions in much criticism of James's work can be dispelled when it is remembered that the kind of experience from which Fleda excludes herself is not in any sense what James understands by the word 'life': 'The life that is in question is simply the extension and refinement of consciousness, of that intelligence which, in Santayana's words "is the highest form of vitality".' L. C. Knights, writing here about *The Beast in the Jungle and Other Stories*,[5] sympathizes with this view for he warns the critics against concentrating 'on the evoked sense of exclusion from experience, without realizing that it is the vitality, the qualities making for life, that the reader has most reason to be grateful for.' James himself puts it slightly differently in the Preface to *What Maisie Knew*: 'The just remark for each of these small exhibited lives is . . . that they are actively, are luxuriously lived. The luxury is that of the number of their moral vibrations, well-nigh unrestricted – not that of an account at the grocer's.' This is, of course, a permissible definition of 'life', but in the light of it, it would be wrong to class Maisie, Nanda

5. *Explorations* (London, 1951).

and Fleda as typical Jamesian innocents. Fleda's passion for renunciation becomes a withdrawal for the purpose of introspective contemplation, and the action she fails to take is unimportant beside the richness of her mental life. Knights is right not to concentrate of the sense of exclusion from experience and the opportunities missed, yet we cannot afford to ignore them altogether, especially when as is the case in *The Spoils of Poynton* the heroine's moral vibrations are obtained and enjoyed at the expense of other lives.

What it comes back to is this: that the isolated consciousness – inasmuch as it is a trapped spectator – cannot provide a vessel for the values associated in James's early work with the ideally civilized sensibility.

The narrator in *The Sacred Fount* provides a good example of the excluded spectator who enjoys the luxury of an espanded consciousness. Why then, in spite of the multitude of his 'moral vibrations', does he represent so signal a failure of James's art? Precisely because of this 'unattached and distressfully uninvolved state.' His lack of immediate and personal involvement in the tragic problems of his fellow guests leads him to treat these problems purely as a challenge to his own intellect and the solutions to them minister not to the lives of those concerned but to his own ego. As he himself puts it: 'I wasn't there to save them. I was there to save my precious pearl.' The metaphor he employs is significant, as James's metaphors always are. The pleasure taken by the narrator in the analysis of the complex moral relationships is throughout of an aesthetic nature, and in this context beauty becomes repellant and the whole preoccupation morbid. James is not unaware of this. He tells us that the price he pays for 'secret success, the lonely liberty and the intellectual joy . . . was the sacrifice of feeling.' There is of course an implicit irony in his over-treatment of the narrator, yet for all that he does indicate, both here and in *The Spoils of Poynton*, that the sacrifice is worth while. In *The Awkward Age* and in *What Maisie Knew* James again makes sacrifices to achieve technical triumphs, but does so without dehumanizing his principal characters, and these two novels are vastly superior to those just discussed.

Although it is primarily by the searching analysis of a condition that is human and universal that they compel our admiration, James is always at pains to trace back the causes of that condition to its roots in a particular arrangement of society. It is by no means wrong, for example, to see *The Awkward Age* and *What Maisie Knew* as drama depicting 'the forces of morality and culture not as stabilized by tradition but as even more dangerous in their workings, their pregnancy of evil and treachery, than in the younger and simpler society. There the idealist, the artist, the innocent or the child may encounter an immanence of disaster even more "ferocious and sinister" than America offers, by reason of the cynicism which time and privilege have bred.'[6] This is one way of characterizing their themes, and one which takes us back, in fact, to the familiar tantalizing relationship between manners and morals – a relationship so well attested that Yvor Winters can with good reason call *The Awkward Age* a tragedy of manners.[7] Certainly there is in these novels a considerable amount of criticism explicitly directed at English society and the effect it may have on the innocence of young, unworldly, but supremely intelligent girls.

We are given in *The Awkward Age* a picture of a witty and sophisticated London clique, presided over by Mrs Brookenham, who must decide whether she can sacrifice her daughter, who is of an age to 'come out', to their free conversation, or whether they must forego the pleasure of their 'good' talk. This is the initial situation and the very fact that it presents a problem, is, James tells us in the Preface, itself a criticism of English manners:

> Nothing comes home more, on the other hand, to the observer of English manners than the very moderate degree to which wise arrangement, in the French sense, of a scientific economy, has ever been invoked; a fact indeed largely explaining the great interest of their incoherence, their heterogeneity, their wild abundance. The French, all analytically, have conceived of fifty diferent proprieties, meeting fifty different cases, whereas the English mind, less intensely at work, has never conceived of but one – the great propriety, for every case, it should in fairness he said, of just being English.

Given these observations, a considerable interest lies in following the independent development of Nanda, who has been given her freedom by Mrs Brookenham, and that of Aggie, her contemporary, who must in the continental manner, until she marries, be kept out of this corrupted and corrupting society. In a novel composed almost entirely of dialogue – 'dialogue organic and dramatic, speaking for itself, representing and embodying substance and form', – such rare passages as the following, helping to guide our responses, must be allowed their full weight. In it James defines for us the essential differences between Aggie and Nanda:

> Since to create a particular little rounded and tinted innocence had been aimed at, the fruit had been grown to the perfection of a peach on a sheltered wall, and this quality of the object resulting from a process might well make him feel himself in contact with something wholly new. Little Aggie differed from any young person he had ever met in that she had been deliberately prepared for consumption and in that, furthermore, the gentleness of her spirit had immensely helped the preparation. Nanda, beside her, was a northern savage, and the reason was partly that the

6. *Craft and Character in Modern Fiction*, by M. D. Zabel (London, 1957).
7. *Maule's Curse* (New York, 1938).

elements of that young lady's nature were already, were publicly, were almost indecorously, active. They were practically there, for good or for ill; experience was still to come and what they might work out to still a mystery; but the sum would get itself done with the figures now on the slate. On Little Aggie's slate the figures were yet to be written, which sufficiently accounted for the difference of the two surfaces. Both the girls struck him as lambs with the great shambles of life in their future; but while one, with its neck in a pink ribbon had no consciousness but that of being fed from the hand with a small sweet biscuit of an objectionable knowledge, the other struggled with instincts and forebodings, with the suspicion of its doom and the far-borne scent, in the flowery fields, of blood. (195–6)

Here then we have the paradox which it is said is always at the centre of tragedy, that what we most admire in the tragic figure, in this case Nanda's superb consciousness, is also that which is the cause of her downfall. In her case the tragedy is even more ironically pointed by the fact that this same consciousness forces upon her the foreknowledge of her fate. Although Mitchy, in love with Nanda, recognizes that this type – 'the modern girl, the product of a hard London whose classic identity with a sheet of white paper has been . . . dropped' – is his real type, this hardly compensates Nanda for the loss of Van, who, more corrupted himself, requires just this kind of blank innocence in his wife.

The word 'corrupt' has been used several times to describe the society in which this drama takes place, and it is a corruption similar to that which characterizes *The Spoils of Poynton* and *The Sacred Fount*. The extension and refinement of that consciousness which is 'the highest form of intelligence', does not seem an adequate basis for a high civilization. Admitted, that the Brookenham's liberal fireside 'cast a wide glow favourable to "real" talk, to play of mind, to an explicit interest in life, a due demonstration of interest by persons qualified to feel it.' And that this meant 'frankness and ease, the perfection, almost, as it were, of intercourse and a tone as far as possible removed from that of the nursery and the schoolroom.' But if this is all to be said for the life described as highly civilized, then one might be excused for believing that it must represent for James an ideal cut down to fit in with a growing cynicism and an awareness of human shortcoming. Indeed, this is the feeling engendered by many passages in *The Awkward Age*. Mrs Brook's salon he appears to sanction, remarking that it fulfils a deep human need, and ignoring the glaring fact that this need is primarily to contrive, to interfere, and generally vulgarly to enjoy the spectacle of human suffering. Edmund Wilson maintains that James 'could never know how we should feel about the gibbering, disembowelled crew who hover about each other with sordid, shadowy designs in *The Awkward*

Age.[8] And though the implication here is not quite just, it is true that we miss in the novel what, from the evidence of James's early work, we might legitimately expect to find in it – an irony that does more than enable us to discriminate between different members of the same group; that, in a word, places once and for all, a witty and sophisticated, but spent and decadent society.

In place of this looked-for irony, James has established criteria which are connected with his technical preoccupations as an artist, and which make for a subsequent thinness in the novels of this period. This can be explained more clearly by reference to *What Maisie Knew*. Here we have a novel in which there is never any doubt about the moral worth of the character, where the values are engraved too strongly to allow of ambiguity, and in which James seems to be overwhelmingly concerned with a world ordered according to a moral system. Indeed, he himself offers us this interpretation in the Preface when he defines Maisie's function as

> . . . bringing people together who would be at least more correctly separate; keeping people separate would be at least more correctly together; flourishing, to a degree, at the cost of many conventions and proprieties, even decencies, really keeping the torch of virtue alive in an air tending infinitely to smother it; really in short, making confusion worse confounded by drawing some fragrance of an ideal across the scent of selfishness, by sowing on barren strands, through the mere fact of presence, the seed of the moral life.

This is an accurate account of how the full irony of Maisie's situation is worked out but, like Zabel's account quoted earlier, it ignores certain undertones which are too elusive to be pinned down by a single quotation, but which James makes more apparent when he says of Maisie that the ugly facts of the story 'by no means constituted the whole appeal', and that about her 'a complexity of life would thus turn to fineness and richness.' She would be saved, he tells us, by becoming, this 'small expanding consciousness', a 'presentable register of impressions, by the experience of certain advantages, by some enjoyed profit and some achieved confidence, rather than coarsened, blurred, sterilized by ignorance and pain.' 'The very principle of her appeal consists', he tells us, 'in her undestroyed freshness . . . in other words that vivacity of intelligence by which she indeed does vibrate in the infected air.' When Mrs Wix accuses Sir Claude of having destroyed Maisie's moral sense he replies, 'on the contrary, I've produced life; it's exquisite, it's sacred.' And this has been James's principle concern, to produce a situation

8. 'The Ambiguity of Henry James' (*Hound and Horn*, Vol. 7, 1934). Wilson's essay is reprinted in *The Question of Henry James*.

. . . in which the child's identity is guarded and preserved, and which makes her case remarkable exactly by the weight of the tax on it, provides distinction for her, provides vitality and variety, through the operation of the tax – which would have done comparatively little for us hadn't it been monstrous. (Preface)

On this the emphasis must be placed, and on its unfortunate correspondence to the situation in *The Sacred Fount*. 'Life', he intimates, however sordid and immoral, can be 'wrought hard, to the hardness of the unforgettable' by the processes of the imagination. It can be given a total value transcending our normal morality. (This of course is what happens in art, and James is quite right to uphold this view against those who would condemn his work as 'painful, unpleasant and disgusting'. But in the novels under discussion, those ideas are applied not to art but to life itself, and life, even the finer essence of it, is open to judgements which have no application to the work of art.) That is to say, to come back to particulars, that Maisie's incorruptibility consists in her ability to extract from the life around her, in the form of a quickened consciousness, a profit which by its very nature is indifferent morally to the facts which call it forth. This profit takes the form of a higher morality able to dispense with the conventional support of a moral sense, and James leaves us in no doubt that he considers Maisie's own morality of a different and finer order than the respectable moral sense represented by Mrs Wix. In an important sense this is true, though it has unfortunate concomitants. Maisie's unique development enables her to discriminate even more surely among the persons who surround her than if her judgements conformed to a conventional pattern. Both Marius Bewley and F. R. Leavis in their long disagreement about this novel say much the same of Maisie, Mr Bewley praising her 'moral[9] intuition' and Leavis her 'moral genius'. They also, in their different ways, recognize that the moral intensity which undoubtedly illumines the novel, throw a peculiar light on the actions of the adults surrounding Maisie. Bewley puts it thus:

> *What Maisie Knew* presents us with a world of horror, but the essence of that horror consists in the way we are able to isolate the grotesqueness of moral evil as it caricatures and distorts human action and motive – to isolate it through the innocent eyes of a little girl whose vision is not sufficiently dulled by conventional experience to absorb the singularity of the irregular world in which she lives.

Leavis in his reply, says:

> There is no hint here of any moral intensity directed upon the sexual misconduct (the context makes that plain) or of enough interest in it as such to lead to moral judgement about it at all. The moral sense that James defines and conveys in this story is that focused in Maisie.

9. Both essays are in *The Complex Fate* (London, 1952).

But neither of them gives this fact the emphasis its importance deserves. To concentrate so fully as James does on the consciousness of his central figure or figures results inevitably in novels in which such criticism of morals and manners as we have, say, in *The Bostonians*, must be sacrificed. Even when we grant everything claimed for the life so masterfully presented in *The Awkward Age* and *What Maisie Knew*, it is still possible to see in it a rootlessness incompatible with the civilization so concretely rendered in *The Europeans* and *Portrait of a Lady*.

James is in pursuit of an ideal of course, and it is one which involves perhaps a completeness he finds lacking in Isabel Archer; one which grarantees, in Matthew Arnold's words, 'the peace and satisfaction which are reached as we draw near to complete spiritual perfection, and not merely to moral perfection, or rather to relative moral perfection.' That James should fail to achieve it would not surprise Arnold, who recognized the difficulty of attaining to 'a human life complete in itself on all sides, and aspiring with all its organs after sweetness, light, and perfection!'

7

The heiress of all
the ages

A desire to tease and elicit from the artist's work a coherent and rounded philosophy – the extracted essence of a lifetime's experience or the painstaking translation into art of another's philosophical system – must be counted one of the major temptations for the literary critic. The temptation is almost irresistible in the case of James's *The Ambassadors*, *The Wings of the Dove* and *The Golden Bowl*, Quentin Anderson's interpretation discussed earlier is only one of many that make the mistake of looking through James's text rather than at it. What these criticisms usually have in common is an insistence that James intends the opposite of what he appears to be saying, or that his words can be made to mean anything at all. Caroline Gordon provides a nice example of this latter fault in her essay tracing archetypal patterns of Christianity in the late novels:

> It is significant, I think, that James turns Mr Verver into a hero with the same gesture he uses to turn Chad into a villain; the characteristic gesture of hands thrust into the pockets.[1]

I propose to set against such interpretative methods a reading which adheres very closely to the text, and one which, following James's own lead, sees in *The Ambassadors* not so much a history of Christianity or a condemnation of self-righteousness, as an appraisal of one man's moral expansion as he comes to the seemingly commonplace recognition that the values enshrined by New England puritanism are inadequate to a proper appreciation of the subtle and various qualities of life in a highly civilized community.

Lambert Strether, a middle-aged American, is sent from Woollett, Mass., by Mrs Newsome, to Paris, in order that he might rescue her son Chad from the immoral life they are both sure he must be leading. Success in this will enable Strether to marry Mrs Newsome and attain the 'consideration and comfort and security' which have so far been lacking in his life. Thus James creates again the familiar pattern of the submission of New World innocence to European

---

1. 'Adam Verver, our National Hero' (*Sewanee Review*, Vol. LXIII, 1955).

experience. Strether proceeds by way of a number of crises to a total view of life' which makes it possible for him finally to 'see' Mrs Newsome and evaluate his own experience. Strether's growing awareness of the 'emptiness' of Woollett and all it stands for is concretely rendered at each stage of his initiation into the life of Paris. The first intimation that there may exist a finer, more intuitive existence than he had hitherto imagined is obliquely introduced by way of an architectural image. James juxtaposes the secondary hotel in which Strether is installed – 'all indoor chill, glass-roofed court and slippery staircase' – with Chad's home:

> High, broad, clear – he was expert enough to make out in a moment that it was admirably built – it fairly embarrassed our friend by the quality that, as he would have said, it 'sprang' on him . . . the quality produced by measure and balance, the fine relation of part to part and space to space, was probably aided by the presence of ornament as positive as it was discreet, and by the complexion of the stone, the cold fair grey, warmed and polished a little by life – neither more nor less than a case of distinction, such a case as he could only feel unexpectedly as a sort of delivered challenge. (I, 85)

One is reminded here of the 'clear white houses' of Roderick Hudson's native New England and how they spoke to Roland Mallett of 'kindness, comfort, safety, the warning voice of duty, the perfect absence of temptation', and also of course the Newport villas in *The Ivory Tower,* and of what they spoke. Roderick Hudson, or rather Mary Garland and her speech on the possibilities for life in Europe, again comes to mind when Strether makes his famous speech to little Bilham, a speech which James reminds us in the Preface contains the 'whole case' of the novel. 'Never can a composition of this sort have sprung straighter from a dropped grain of suggestion.' The essence of *The Ambassadors* is, he says, contained in the following exhortation:

> 'Live all you can; it's a mistake not to. It doesn't so much matter what you do in particular, so long as you have your life. If you haven't had that what have you had? . . .. I see it now. I haven't done so enough before – and now I'm old; too old at any rate for what I see.' (I, 190)

This is the vision to which Strether eventually comes. It is the 'precious moral' of everything, and the interest lies largely in Strether's attempts to retain that vision in the face of any shock that might swing him back to 'the principles of Woollett'. This shock comes when he discovers by accident that Chad and Madame de Viommet are lovers, and they act out for him the lie 'in the charming affair'. However, his experience has fitted him now to approach such facts in a new way and his vision remains essentially unimpaired. He has participated in and contributed to 'life', by becoming 'with his perceptions and his mistakes, his concessions and his reserves, the droll mixture, as it must seem to them, of his braveries and his fears, the general spectacle of his art and his innocence . . . a common priceless ground for them to meet upon.' If one's moral vibrations are the test of life, then Strether has lived, and the fact of his having done so and the importance James attaches to this point make nonsense of Quentin Anderson's contention that 'Strether is the worst of us all'.

So it is that Lambert Strether is on the side of 'life' and the novel is, in Philip Rahv's words, 'a veritable declaration of the rights of man – not, to be sure, of the rights of the public or the social man, but of the rights of the private man, of the rights of personality, whose openness to experience provides the sole effective guaranty of its development.'[2] What remains to be examined is the actual quality of the experience to which Strether submits himself, and the role of the individual consciousness which becomes in the late novels the ground for the testing of all values. These considerations are forced upon us by the subtleties of the late manner, which for some critics at least represents a 'doing' disproportionate to the issues – 'to any issues that are concretely held and presented.'[3] Before embarking on an extended analysis of James's technique in *The Ambassadors* I want to place the concept of consciousness in its historical perspective. This will serve the dual purpose of clarifying James's relation to the civilization coming into being during his lifetime, and free him from the artificial ties with which Quentin Anderson seeks to bind him to his father. It may also throw a little light on the way in which, as James becomes more immersed in the presentation of individual consciousnesses, he comes to rely more and more on the power of myth and symbol.

Emerson, in his essay *The Transcendentalist*, affirms the overriding importance of consciousness:

> The idealist takes his departure from his consciousness, and reckons the world an appearance . . . [he] has another measure, which is metaphysical, namely, the rank which things themselves take in his consciousness; not at all the size or appearance. Mind is the only reality, of which men and all other natures are better or worse reflectors. Nature, literature, history are only subjective phenomena. (*Miscellanies*)

This last view he illustrates at some length in his essay, *History*:

> The world exists for the education of each man. There is no age or state of society or mode of action in history, to which there is not somewhat

2. *Image and Idea* (London, 1957).
3. F. R. Leavis in *The Great Tradition* argues the case against the late novels much more persuasively than does Maxwell Geismar in *Henry James and his Cult* (London, 1964).

corresponding in his life. Everything tends in a wonderful manner to abbreviate itself and yield its own virtue to him. He should see that he can live all history in his own person. He must sit solidly at home, and not suffer himself to be bullied by kings or empires, but know that he is greater than all the geography and all the government of the world; he must transfer the point of view from which history is commonly read, from Rome and Athens and London to himself, and not deny his conviction that he is the court, and if England or Egypt have anything to say to him, he will try the case; if not, let them for ever be silent. He must attain and maintain that lofty site where facts yield their secret sense, and poetry and annals are alike.

And Thoreau, who retired to the woods in order to 'suck out all the marrow of life', maintained that: 'if I am overflowing with life, am rich in experience for which I lack expression, then nature will be my language full of poetry – all nature will fable and every natural phenomenon be a myth.' As he elsewhere says, 'A fact truly and absolutely stated . . . acquires a mythologic or universal significance.' The world as appearance – the poetic and symbolic content of historical fact – and the impressionistic use of these facts all suggest the late novels; the James who, at the very end of his life, became obsessed by the figure of Napoleon, and who images states of consciousness in the language of great public events:

> Strether had all along been subject to sudden gusts of fancy in connection with such matters as these – odd starts of the historic sense, superstitions and divinations with no warrant but their intensity. Thus and so, on the eve of the great recorded dates, the days and nights of revolution, the sounds had come in, the omens, the beginnings broken out. They were the smell of revolution, the smell of the public temper, or perhaps simply the smell of blood. (II, 246)

Even when James appears to be disagreeing with the Transcendentalists view of the world, he does so in imagery curiously akin to theirs. Consider for example these two passages, one taken from *The Ambassadors*, and the other from Emerson's essay, *The Transcendentalist*:

> The affair – I mean the affair of life – couldn't, no doubt, have been different for me; for it's at the best a tin mould, either fluted or embossed, with ornamental excrescences, or else smooth and dreadfully plain, into which, the helpless jelly, one's consciousness is poured – so that one 'takes' the form, as the great cook says. (II, 191)

> I – this thought which is called I – is the mould into which the world is poured like melted wax. The mould is invisible, but the world betrays the shape of the mould.

There is, I think, ample evidence firmly to establish James's dependence, not on his father's unique Swedenborgian system, but on the native intellectual climate of which they both partook.

There is of course another side to James's preoccupation with what he called 'the essence of life'. In an important sense he is a product of the trend discussed elsewhere – the trend in a mass society to the isolation of the individual. R. P. Blackmur has discussed the plight of this individual whose consciousness, he says, we burden beyond our previous measure: 'We make him in our art, especially the art of literature, assume the whole weight of the cultural establishment . . . . There is only the succession of creative consciousnesses – each of which is an attempt to incorporate, to give body to, to incarnate, as much as it is possible to experience, to feel it, the life of the times.'[4] All the main characteristics of James's late fiction derive from the attempt to dramatize such consciousnesses.

In spite of the profound disgust he felt for the conditions of production on the English stage James was always attracted by the idea of playwriting, believing that 'the drama is the ripest of all the arts.' As early as 1882 he recorded his resolve to delay no longer: 'After long years of waiting, of obstruction, I find myself able to put into execution the most cherished of all my projects, that of beginning to work for the stage.'[5]

The period of his greatest involvement with the theatre was not extensive and though his plays were at best lukewarm successes and did nothing to bolster his literary reputation, the legacy of these attempts to create dramatic works was a conception of fictional form that affected everything he subsequently produced. If it is going too far to say the he now developed an entirely new idea of form (for it was presumably because he had arrived at some concept of dramatic structure that he decided to embark upon a series of plays in the first place) then at least one can maintain that his experiments in a different mode considerably deepened his insights into the nature of dramatic economy. Very early in his career he thought he had mastered the techniques of the French playwrights Sardou and Augier, and said as much in one of his letters to William, but nothing teaches the rudiments of a craft like having to grapple with its special problems for oneself, and by comparison with his fiction of the 1890s and later, *The Bostonians* and *The Princess Casamassima* look almost like the loose and baggy monsters he came to despise so much. On the other hand, it is surely wrong to suggest, as does Austin Warren, that James came to depend upon the use of dramatic, neo-classical structure in his later work.[6] For all the use of balance and symmetry in *The Golden Bowl*, and the careful distribution of compositional masses in *The Wings of The Dove* and *The Ambassadors*, these novels

4. *The Lion and the Honeycomb* (London, 1957).
5. *The Notebooks of Henry James*, ed. By F. O. Matthiessen and Kenneth B. Murdock (New York, 1947).
6. 'Myth and Dialectic in the Later Novels' (Kenyon Review, Vol. V, 1943).

nevertheless represent themes that have been 'completely expressed'. By most standards the subjects of these later novels are very large and complex and we should not complain if they have received proportionately massive treatment. What one can complain about justly is the treatment James lavishes on the relatively small and intractable themes which are at the heart of *The Sacred Fount* and to a lesser extent *The Awkward Age* and *What Maisie Knew*. The relationships in these earlier novels of the 1890s are capable of extension or intensification only by the expedients James worked so furiously: duplication, incremental repetition, parallelism and the rest.

It can be argued that even in *The Ambassadors*, James's determination to maintain the essential action within the range of Strether's consciousness leads him into unnecessary difficulties of presentation. Any weaknesses and potential weaknesses that the novel has, result from a failure to effect a complete fusion of subject and method such as there is in *The Wings of the Dove* and *The Golden Bowl*. In order to get his story told without 'going behind' any of the other characters, James is forced to contrive a skein of connective tissue which will allow Strether, and the reader, to gather necessary information from carefully planted ficelles. James's chief prop, Maria Gostrey, in particular needs to have an encyclopaedic knowledge of the people Strether is interested in, so that he can always be apprised of the relevant background to existing relationships. And where such knowledge is unavailable Maria falls back on her positive genius for intuitive insight to fill in the gaps while still avoiding the platitude of flat statement. More dangerous, though, to the novel's form, is the general narrative procedure James is forced into by his decision to keep the action all within Strether's awareness without giving in to the inevitable looseness of first-person narrative. The characteristic development of the subject follows a basic pattern from which James finds it difficult to escape. After each of what he calls his 'greater turns', Strether withdraws from the world of Chad and Madame de Vionnet to where Maria 'so faithfully awaited him', and together they proceed to pick over the latest events in the drama. Then, as a prelude to his next sortie, Strether is commonly left to brood alone on past and future developments. The reiteration of this structural pattern could make for tedium when the novel is read continuously, though as a solution to the problem of twelve-part serial publication, James's methods make those of other nineteenth-century novelists – even Dickens – seem very crude indeed. The difference is that James acknowledges the danger and treats it; uses it, in fact, to achieve a genuine *progression d'effet*. This is the mark of his maturity as a novelist. In his earliest fiction an insistence upon the moral significance of his themes led him to overlook the possibilities for dramatic economy in the material; while in his middle period when he carried on a long flirtation with aestheticism, slight themes were made to bear a weight of over-complex, baroque, fictional designs. The fusions achieved in his last novels were not accomplished without a good deal of hard preparation.

Both *The American* and *What Maisie Knew* afford good oportunities for examining the development and assimilation of the dramatic technique of *The Ambassadors*. Not only do the events and the characters of *The Ambassadors* duplicate many of those in *The American*, but also James came back to his early novel in 1890 and made of it a four-act play which had a brief run on the London stage. What makes comparison with *What Maisie Knew* interesting on the other hand, is not its subject so much as the way in which James depicts the dichotomy between the world as it exists and Maisie's developing awareness of it.

The Ambassadors demonstrates perfectly the truth of James's remark that the constant opposition of picture and scene can make for an intensity more dramatic than the merely dramatic, and for an elasticity that makes the novel the most prodigious of literary forms. For the complete absence of such intensity one need look no further than the first chapter of *The American*. Like any one of several dozen nineteenth-century novelists James immediately unloads upon his reader a welter of geographical, historical, physiological and moral facts which serve to place his hero definitively, and effectively prevent the possibility of any further development on his part. Christopher Newman's circumstances, history and person are catalogued in the manner of Scott or Stendhal, and the first two monumentally daunting paragraphs are rounded off with a neat little list of antithetical qualities which we are asked to notice in 'our friend's eye': 'Frigid and yet friendly, frank yet cautious, shrewd yet credulous, positive yet skeptical, confident yet shy, extremely intelligent and extremely goodhumoured, there was something vaguely defiant in its concessions, and something profoundly reassuring in its reserve.' In case any of this is lost on the reader he is finally reminded even more flatly that: 'Decision, salubrity, jocosity, prosperity seemed to hover within his call.' Eventually James sets Newman free to act but, carrying as he does already such a large, well-defined character and history, it is not surprising that his scene with Noemie Nioche, which makes up the rest of the first chapter, fails altogether in dramatic intensity. Our awareness of the manipulating hand of the novelist is too strong at this point to concede to Newman the necessary freedom of independent action. The scene would have been a weak one in any event though. The flatness of the two first descriptive paragraphs is exactly matched by the extensive, almost uninterrupted dialogue which follows it. Merely to alternate passages of narration with scenes of dialogue, no matter how accurate the description or penetrating the conversation, is really to deny that the novel has a unique form at all. The novelist's function, as James himself was later to insist, is to mediate between his material and his audience, not to pop up between scenes for exhibition like a puppet-master.

The first chapter of *The Ambassadors*, like that of *The American*, introduces us to the novel's hero newly embarked on a visit to Europe, and as all first chapters must, serves some of the same purposes as the one we have just been looking at: the establishment of mood, tone, and general style, and the laying down of very basic themes, together with the provision of a certain minimum of information. The immeasurably greater expressiveness and economy of *The Ambassadors* is partly the result of a more flexible prose style, but more important than this is the general method whereby dialogue is as descriptive as description is acutely analytic, where Strether's luminous consciousness, reducing everything to subjection, lends an added dimension, a double function to every object, gesture, and conversational nuance.

Ian Watt's analysis of *The Ambassadors'* first paragraph[7] demonstrates the stylistic complexity of a prose seeking to follow the movements of Strether's involved thought processes. The verbal idiosyncrasies he particularly singles out are a preference for non-transitive verbs, a heavy use of abstract nouns and of the word 'that', the presence of a great many negatives and near negatives, and the use of elegant variation to avoid the reiteration of personal pronouns and adjectives. All these characteristics, Watt points out, testify to an abatement of the active subject-verb-object sequence, and to an actuality which has been subjected to mental process. Nearly all the characteristic elements of this prose are present even in the first sentence: 'Strether's first question, when he reached the hotel, was about his friend: yet on his learning that Waymarsh was apparently not to arrive till evening he was not wholly disconcerted.' It is an extremely active, cerebral style: tentative, circling, and oblique. Yet seen in the retrospect of the entire novel the sentence is full of anticipatory meanings; just as the complacent, inert naturalness of the first sentence in *The American* testifies, if in a more negative fashion, to that novel's subject: 'On a brilliant day in May, in the year 1868, a gentleman was reclining at his ease on the great circular divan which at that period occupied the centre of the *salon carré* in the museum of the Louvre.' Though his natural complacency will be

7. 'The First Paragraph of *The Ambassadors:* An Explication' (Essays in Criticism, Vol. X, 1960). The style of *The Ambassadors* is also discussed by David Lodge in *Language of Fiction* (London, 1966), and by Seymour Chatman in *The Later Style of Henry James* (London, 1972).

somewhat shaken, Europe will remain almost as a museum for Christopher Newman, and he will at the end be left at least with his moral ease, even if he is to be deprived of the chief comfort of his life. To read all these signs in the first sentence of *The American* is, however, an act of fancy, whereas in *The Ambassadors*, not to see the relation of Strether's first question to all the others he must ask, and the feelings with which he responds, as an essential indication of the complicated ambivalence with which his mission inspires him, would be to do less than justice to the subtlety of James's art.

Some of the characteristics of the later prose can be seen displacing the flatness of mere statement in the revisions James made for the New York edition of *The American*. He did not change the first two paragraphs radically; nothing short of re-writing the whole novel could have produced the kind of effect achieved by *The Ambassadors*. But within the limits he allowed himself he brought about some instructive changes. By a displacement of the more usual and somewhat repetitive subject-predicate relation found in the earlier version, by the use of ellipsis, compression and abstraction, James manages to vary the insistent pattern of description and suggest at the same time a less wooden figure than Newman had hitherto seemed. Of course James's revisions were not uniformly happy. In his efforts to avoid the worn banalities of character drawing and to substitute the vivid picture for the conventional phrase he occasionally produced the ludicrous, as in the passage where the phrase 'he was clean shaved' is rendered as 'he spoke, as to cheek and chin, of the joys of the matutinal steel.' In the dialogue with Noemie which follows, James's revisions make the most of his ability to render speech witty and colloquial, and as far as is possible he brings to life this unpromising scene. The structure of the chapter as a whole, though, remains as it was – inert and stiff. Comparison with *The Ambassadors* exhibits its lack of vitality.

James had proved in *The Awkward Age* that he could write really constructive dialogue: 'dialogue organic and dramatic, speaking for itself, representing and embodying substance and form', but such a *tour de force* as *The Awkward Age* had about as little to do with the art of fiction as obstacle races have to do with athletics. Of course a novelist must be able to write speeches that do more than merely distinguish one character from the next, and of course dialogue does make for organic structure, at least in James's novels it does when it is not being used merely to develop a richness of texture. But in the last analysis what one values the novel for are the things it accomplishes that are not possible on the stage. In *The Ambassadors*, just as the structural interest comes from the juxtaposition of scene and picture the real thickening of the texture occurs not only in the conversations, but also in the silences which enfold them, silences which are almost entirely absent from *The American*. In the earlier novel action often seems to be quite unrelated to perceptible motive; certainly James himself does nothing to strengthen the necessary connection for the reader, and this largely accounts for the romanticism which James in his Preface attributes to the improbability of the Bellegardes' way of rejecting Christopher Newman. Of course their actions are improbable but no more so than those of Kate Croy and Merton Densher in *The Wings of The Dove*. In the stage version of *The American*, the substitution of action for analysis makes for even less probability. In order to tighten the structure of events James resorts to drastic foreshortening and excision, and in the process his characters are reduced to mere caricatures. An examination of one brief encounter will be enough to show what has been sacrificed.

In the novel, Mrs Tristram stands in almost exactly the same relation to Claire as Maria Gostrey does to Madame Vionnet in *The Ambassadors*, and it is she who pushes Newman into relation with the young aristocrat, inasmuch as she divines what lies at the back of Newman's visit to Europe and consequently offers herself to him as a matchmaker. The scene in which she does this is one in which it would have been easy for James to strike the wrong note. The crudity and vulgarity of their discussion in which Newman has to declare his intention of perching a beautiful women on his pile 'like a statue on a monument' is cleverly treated by having Tom Tristram present to forestall and undercut the reader's direct response with his own ironic commentary on their conversation. To the speech in which Newman announces himself anxious to acquire for a wife 'the best article on the market', Tom Tristram responds more quickly than his wife:

'Why didn't you tell a fellow all this at the outset?' Tristram demanded. 'I've been trying so to make you fond of *me*!'

'It's remarkably interesting,' said Mrs Tristam. 'I like to see a man who knows his own mind.' . . .

'Have you any objections to a foreigner?' Mrs Tristram continued, addressing their friend, who had tilted back his chair and, with his feet on a bar of the balcony railing and his hands in his pockets, sat looking at the stars.

'No Irish need apply,' said Tristram. (36)

In the later novels James avoids the flatness of direct commitment more subtly than this by carefully preparing all his scenes in advance, devoting time to the exploration of the mental states of the participants. Where this resource is not available to him, as in the stage version of *The American*, and he also refuses to utilize reflectors like Tom Tristram, he is reduced to broad comedy or crude melodrama.

In the play the corresponding scene, in which Newman's desire for a wife is broached, takes place with M. Mioche. Newman has just been introduced to Valentin and he is attempting to learn something more about him:

Nioche: My profession is to answer questions, and it's to my honour that none have ever been asked me to which I haven't instantly produced a reply. For instance I can go straight through the great house of Bellegarde.

(*Puts bottle down by fire.*)

Newman: The great house of Bellegarde?

Nioche: The relations of my noble guest. It's true there are very few left today – that makes it easy. Only his mother, his elder brother and his beautiful sister.

Newman: (*Who has been looking at a book on the table, right, here turns quickly, leg up on chair.*)

Has he got a beautiful sister?

Nioche: As beautiful as an old picture – some delicate pastel – and a saint into the bargain.

Newman: That's just what I want to see!

(*Quickly taking out again his memorandum book.*)

Her name, please?

Nioche: (*importantly*) Madame La Contessa Claire de Cintré.

Newman: Dammit Neo – she's *married*?

Nioche: She was sir; but that's all over. She's now an elegant young widow.

Newman: (*jotting down*) That's just what I want to see!

(*He sits in chair, right, and with his legs stretched well out, takes notes as Nioche speaks.*)

(*Complete Plays,* 200)

It has been argued that James was here quite deliberately trying to portray Newman with broad comic possibilities, but this view is hardly consistent with his rather shamefaced announcement to William in 1892 – two years after the play's first appearance – that he had written an entirely new Act for it 'in a comedy-sense – heaven forgive me'. His original conception of *The American* may be partly inferred from this letter: 'So the fourth is now *another* fourth, which will basely gratify their artless instincts and British thick-wittedness and thanks to it the poor play will completely save one's honour.'

James was to find that as he developed his characteristic techniques he had to prune away the number of events in his novels in order to give himself space to create a workable surface. It is difficult to understand though, why, in 1890, he chose to keep in *The American* the more expendable Noemie and her father at the expense of the seemingly more useful Mrs Tristram; unless he was tempted to do so by the success on the French stage of a long procession of similar courtesans from Camille to Olympe. Whatever his motive, the consequent complications of the plot prevent him from treating any of the resulting relationships fully. He was to practise a much stricter economy in *The Ambassadors*, and later still in *The Golden Bowl* and *The Ivory Tower* James came at last to deny himself all the irrelevant luxuries he indulged in in his early work. In fiction, as in drama, complication by way of simple addition involves one ultimately in the use of a *deus ex machina* to achieve at best a factitious resolution, whereas the development which proceeds logically by means of assimilation and analysis, entails its own right resolution.

It is with the techniques of assimilation and analysis in the first chapter of *The Ambassadors* that I want now to deal. Even before Strether meets Maria Gostrey in the hotel at Chester and arranges to accompany her around the town, we are in possession of a good deal of information about the nature of his visit to Europe, and more importantly, his feelings about this and about his fellow-countryman Waymarsh. So that when he does hold the briefest of discussions with Maria about their mutual acquaintance Waymarsh, James can claim much more weight for their conversation; is able, in fact, to hint at the reciprocal clutch at the faint connotation with complete plausibility: 'It was as if a good deal of talk had already passed. They even vaguely smiled at it.' Similarly, Because he defers any description of Strether's person until after the meeting with Maria, he is able to use it when it does come to help characterize Maria too, ending his description of the items of Strether's facial furniture with the words: 'which an attentive observer would have seen to be catalogued, on the spot, in the vision of the other party to Strether's appointment.' If Maria's taxonomic skill can be employed so economically, then Strether's lack of it can also be made to serve a double purpose; his description of Maria testifying to his intent but untutored vision: 'She had, this lady, a perfect plain propriety, an expensive subdued suitability, that her companion was not free to analyse, but that struck him, so that his consciousness of it was instantly acute, as a quality quite new to him.'

At this point James suspends the action of the novel for a moment longer with Strether standing on the lawn of the hotel, ostensibly feeling in the pocket of his overcoat for something, but in fact employing this stratagem to delay his imminent meeting with Maria whilst he ruminates on the feeling that 'he was launched in something of which the sense would be quite disconnected from the sense of his past.' His subsequent attempt to analyse his own inadequacy and to account for Maria's superior civilization represent for him the first steps in an investigative process which will gradually become more and more intense under the tutelage of Maria herself. In the first few pages of the novel where the first real scene between them is being prepared, some of the characteristic features of the novel's structure are rehearsed. Of course there has been as yet no development of the main subject, so that the material upon which Strether muses, both with and without Maria's help, has to be improvised. But it is just this creative ingenuity whereby the groundwork of the novel is incorporated dramatically into the fabric of the action that is so remarkable.

The following scene is written with a deliberateness which would in all probability have been wasted were it not for the careful preparation preceding it. After James has described his characters and after they have carefully scrutinized and pondered over each other, they are at last allowed to present themselves directly, giving the reader a third, ironic view of the two expatriates in their defensive self-analysis. This is not the only function of the scene though: there is more to the chapter than mere portraiture. At the very beginning, Strether's feelings of ambivalence about his meeting with Waymarsh are given as an indication that his relation to his actual errand might prove to be not simple, and throughout the chapter his submission to the beauty of the Roman town and his nagging fear that in his enjoyment he has been neglecting his duty, provide a subtle introduction to the novel's theme:

> All sorts of other pleasant small things – small things that were yet large for him – flowered in the air of the occasion; but the bearing of the occasion itself on matters still remote concerns us too closely to permit us to multiply our illustrations. Two or three, however, in truth, we should perhaps regret to lose. The tortuous wall – girdle, long since snapped, of the little swollen city, half held in place by careful civic hands – wanders, in narrow file, between parapets smoothed by peaceful generations, pausing here and there for a dismantled gate or a bridged gap, with rises and drops, steps up and steps down, queer twists, queer contacts, peeps into homely streets and under the brows of gables, views of cathedral tower and waterside fields, of huddled English town and ordered English country. Too deep almost for words was the delight of these things for Strether; yet as deeply mixed with it were certain images of his inward picture. He had trod this walk in the far-off time at twenty-five; but that, instead of spoiling it, only enriched it for present feeling and marked his renewal as a thing substantial enough to share. It was with Waymarsh he should have shared it, and he was now, accordingly, taking from him something that was his due. (I, 14)

So the central scene, by virtue of James's careful preparation, gains immeasurably in meaning and serves to prefigure the main action. Strether's nervousness, exacerbated by his neglect of Waymarsh, has been indicated throughout by his obsessive attention to his watch, and when he drags it out for the sixth time Maria can't resist observing:

'You're really in terror of him.'
He smiled a smile that he almost felt to be sickly.
'Now you can see why I'm afraid of you.'
'Because I've such illuminations? Why, they're all for your help! It's what I told you,' she added, 'just now. You feel as if this were wrong.'
He fell back once more, settling himself, as if to hear more about it, against the parapet. 'Then get me out!' Her face fairly brightened for the joy of the appeal, but, as if it were a question of immediate action, she visibly considered. 'Out of waiting for him? – of seeing him at all?'
'Oh no – not that,' said poor Strether, looking grave.
'I've got to wait for him, and I want very much to see him. But out of the terror. You did put your finger on it a few minutes ago. It's general, but it avails itself of particular occasions. That's what it's doing for me now. I'm always considering something else; something else, I mean, than the thing of the moment. The obsession of the other thing is the terror. I'm considering at present, for instance, something else than *you*.'
She listened with charming earnestness. 'Oh, you oughtn't to do that!'
'It's what I admit. Make it, then, impossible.'
She continued to think. 'Is it really an "order" from you? – that I shall take the job? *Will* you give yourself up?'
Poor Strether heaved his sigh. 'If I only could! But that's the deuce of it – that I never can. No – I can't.'
She was not, however, discouraged. 'But you desire to, at least!'
'Oh, unspeakably!'
'Ah then, if you'll try!' (I, 17–18)

The process by which Strether gives himself up is of course the very heart of the novel.

My first Part or two are expository, presentative (on these lines of present picture and movement), and are primar(il)y concerned with his encounter and relation with two persons his portrayed intercourse with whom throws up to the surface what it concerns us to learn.[8]

James's willingness to expend 20,000 words on initial, explanatory matter, testifies to his desire for the kind of 'solidity of specification' he had failed to provide in *The American*.

In actual fact, the exposition proper can hardly be said to begin

8. James's Project for *The Ambassadors* in *The Notebooks of Henry James*.

until the second part, much of the first being given over to what James calls 'a slight and comparatively subordinate feature of my business . . . the exhibition of the two men as affected in wholly different ways by an experience considerably identical.' Originally he had intended to bring Strether and Waymarsh together immediately and only then introduce Maria. Had he kept to this plan, the comparison between the two men would have lost much of its force and the scene *would* have been a subordinate feature. His decision to reverse the meetings not only makes for an opening with greater dramatic possibilities, but also shifts the initial emphasis to the novel's central theme: Strether's own quickened response to the stimulus of Europe. By delaying Waymarsh's appearance until after the first encounter with Maria, James transforms what was primarily a comic scene into one having an organic connection with the rest of the novel; its laconic directness balancing and enhancing the complexities of the first chapter. Even such details as the stroll by moonlight add something to the changed atmosphere brought about by Waymarsh's presence, Strether's dream of romantic effects being merged in his friend's mundane regret for the absence of thicker overcoats. But the chief contrasts are more directly associated with Waymarsh himself. Strether is stuck by his friend's almost wilful discomfort in Europe, and sees that this habit of disapprobation, or at least the despair of felicity could 'constitute a menace for his own prepared, his already confirmed, consciousness of the agreeable.' Waymarsh's dogged, silent rectitude, apparent in his stiff posture no less than in his unhappy history briefly outlined in this chapter, represents then, an important element in the story. He is a constant, if extreme reminder in the early part of the novel of the pressures from Woollett, Massachusetts, which prevent Strether himself from succumbing too readily to his consciousness of the agreeable.

The symmetry of these two chapters which might be supposed to give the novel's opening too schematic an appearance, is in fact mitigated by the variety of methods James uses in the creation of oppositions. His subtle modifications of the proportion of scene to picture in particular, while allowing him to present Waymarsh in a more direct fashion than Maria, also serve to give the opening a greater density than it would otherwise have had.

A further alleviation is provided by Chapter 3, the last in Part I. Here James brings his three characters together, and in a final stroll around the old town allows Strether a series of presentiments. This is, as he later remembers it, 'the very climax of his foretaste,' yet for all its compact meaningfulness it is rendered with a buoyancy entirely appropriate to these early scenes. Waymarsh's grim, ambiguous, glumness when faced with the wicked old rows of Chester is contrasted with Strether's immediate, lively response to everything.

Even Waymarsh's interest in what James calls 'the merely useful trades' is turned to account, inasmuch as it distinguishes him from Strether, who 'flaunted an affinity with the dealers in stamped letter-paper and in neckties' while his companion occupied himself with the windows of iron-mongers and saddlers. Finally, when Waymarsh can no longer bear what Maria and Strether represent for him – the multiplication of shibboleths and the discrimination of types and tones, he seeks his freedom in a nearby jeweller's shop, asserting himself in what James had come to think of as a typically American way, by buying up the objects he can possess in no other way. This 'sacred rage' of Waymarsh's, provoked in him by his companion's remorseless analysis, is something which animates not only Waymarsh, but Mrs Newsome and Sarah Pocock too. It is the chief constituent of the New England philosophy of life as James presents it here, and it is against this simple, moralistic outlook that Strether has to fight to gain his new, complex, vision.

The oblique approach to a subject in Part I, gives way in the second part to a method which, if less intrinsically interesting from a structural point of view, demonstrates better the kind of opposition between picture and scene which gives the novel its unique poise. If anything Part II is an oversimplification of the novel's method; the first chapter, a scene between Strether and Maria at a London theatre in which Strether's mission is fully outlined, being balanced exactly by a second chapter of reflections where Strether broods upon his own past, passively inviting comparisons between his early life and that he supposes Chad Newsome to be enjoying now. In this way we are given a more subjective evaluation of his business in Paris. The symmetry of the two chapters is insisted upon not only by the similarity of subject matter and the juxtaposition of dialogue and narration, but also by their matching shape and size. Each has a few pages of preparation, locating the episode in space and time followed by, in the one case, almost uninterrupted dialogue, and in the other a long unbroken series of reflections. While such a simple structuring of material is seldom found again in the novel, James is only doing here what he continues to do throughout, giving us first a fairly objective presentation of the situation and then Strether's more complex sense of it. The structural devices used in *The Ambassadors*, while allowing some flexibility in their exploitation, have as their primary aim 'the entire expression' of a difficult subject. In the novels preceding it, on the other hand, James appears to be using complex structures not to express but to contrive difficult subjects. In his Preface to *What Maisie Knew*, for example, he talks of his idea that the complexity of life around her should turn for Maisie into fineness, but in the novel itself the complexities of life are sacrificed to the involutions of art; parallelism and the accumulation of branching connections being substituted for the patient exploration of a properly constituted relationship. Maisie's fineness is the product of imperviousness, Strether's of complete awareness. In *The Ambassadors* appearances are probed and probed until the centre is reached upon which Strether's new vision is founded, but in *What Maisie Knew* there is no middle ground between the world of appearance and the abysses beyond it. Maisie's value as an 'ironic centre' depends on the immaturity of her vision which confines her almost completely to the surface of things:

> She was taken into the confidence of passions on which she fixed just the stare she might have had for images bounding across the wall in the slide of a magic lantern. Her little world was phantasmagoric – strange shadows bouncing on a sheet. It was as if the whole performance had been given for her – a mite of a half-scared infant in a great dim theatre. (21)

Maisie's shadow world with its hint of a lurking evil behind it may be contrasted with this famous metaphor which is used to present Strether's first sense of Paris:

> It hung before him this morning, a vast bright Babylon, like some huge iridescent object, a jewel brilliant and hard, in which parts were not to be discriminated nor differences comfortably marked. It twinkled and trembled and melted together, and what seemed all surface one moment seemed all depths the next. (I, 78–9)

Strether's consciousness of these depths, however vague, is a guarantee of his development, and it is on this that attention is focused. In Maisie's case, although James emphatically claims in his Preface that the ugly facts of the story 'by no means constituted the whole appeal' of the subject for him, the limited value of Maisie's perceptions does necessarily send the reader back for interest to the intricate movements of her elders' extra-marital manoeuvres.

E. M. Forster calls *The Ambassadors* a dance. *What Maisie Knew* is more like one. Even stated in bare outline the design of the plot has the regularity associated with more formal arts. The story opens when Beale and Ida Farange are separated by divorce yet kept in tenuous relation by Maisie who alternates in six-monthly stints between her parents' new establishments. They both quickly re-marry and their respective spouses are themselves brought by Maisie into a relationship which eventually becomes intimate, and which, in a neat reversal of the situation at the novel's beginning, depends upon Maisie for its continuance. In the meantime her parents are seen to be separately declining in almost geometric progression as they take up with a succession of more and more ugly and vulgar, sexual partners. The end of the novel, and the end of Maisie's childhood, come when she cuts herself free from her step-parents' affair, demonstrating in her final choice the birth of her moral sense.

James takes pains not only to make the careers of Maisie's parents run almost exactly parallel courses, but by presenting them in scenes which duplicate the organization of each other even in small details, ensures that every act will be corrosively underlined. This parallelism, along with the complication of relationships entailed by it, and the necessary simplification of minor characters, even to the point of caricature, are all techniques reminiscent of Restoration Comedy. In its general outline *What Maisie Knew* is more like *The Way of the World* than *Olympe's Marriage* or the other French plays James studied so assiduously.

The transgressions of Maisie's parents are depicted with James's usual sense of economy in dramatically charged scenes to which Maisie is a frightened but not inactive witness. Two of these in particular, serving to precipitate the final coalitions of the novel, demonstrate their dependence on the drama. They both take place in public, as if flagrantly to proclaim her parents' misdemeanours, one in Kensington Gardens and the other at an Earls Court Exhibition. In the first Maisie has been strolling along the banks of the Serpentine with her stepfather, Sir Claude, when they suddenly, at a turn in the walk, encounter Ida Farange, Maisie's mother and Sir Claude's wife, who they thought was in Belgium playing billiards. She is out with her latest lover the captain, and there is a moment of sordidly comic confusion when Maisie mistakes Ida's companion for one of her earlier lovers, Lord Eric, and Sir Claude takes him for yet another, the Count. While Sir Claude and Ida stand 'face to face in hatred' indulging themselves in mutual recrimination, Maisie is left with the captain, ironically exposing the degradation of her mother's life in her innocent eulogies of her.

The scene which helps to stylize this one by duplication, stands in close proximity to it, separated by only a short, non-scenic chapter transferring the action to her stepmother and setting up the scene at the Exhibition. Mrs Beale has taken Maisie there in the hope of meeting Sir Claude. Instead they come upon her husband with a brand-new mistress whom Mrs Beale thinks must be a Mrs Cudden, but who turns out to be an American countess. After a moment of violent shock and confusion which is not described in detail, Maisie is whisked away by her father to the countess's house. The countess herself, who according to Beale has a horror of vulgar scenes, had disappeared as soon as the shouting started, and as they wait for her, Beale tells Maisie of his plan to leave for America and effectively sever his connection with her for good. This latter part of the scene goes beyond mere repetition of the Kensington Gardens episode and carries the plot forward a little. But within two chapters James has restored the pattern completely with an identically shaped scene, in which Maisie's mother in turn breaks off her relation with her daughter by announcing her imminent departure for South Africa.

These complicated gyrations are, of course, meant to allow scope for the operation of a heavy structural irony, and even though Maisie is not always a fine enough instrument to register the ironies of a given situation, in the matter of creating aesthetic perspective *What Maisie Knew* represents a significant advance on *The Way of the World* where, even though Congreve makes use of reflectors, it is primarily his witty verbal texture that gives him latitude for his slick equivocations; or on James's own earlier novel *The Sacred Fount*, in which he appears to be fully implicated himself in the morbid world he has created. In so far as *What Maisie Knew* is a failure, it represents James's inability to maintain strict concentricity. In a novel of this kind everything must be held together by a commanding centre or interest will be dissipated towards the periphery. The development of Maisie's moral sense and the choice she makes in the final scene – a scene towards which everything else should be tending – is unfortunately subordinated to the exhibition of the workings of her precocious mind, so that the reader is never quite sure of the novel's precise focus.

James never seems to be in danger of falling into the same errors in *The Ambassadors*. Where Beale and Ida Farange reveal themselves in their progressive deterioration as they alternately make and break the patterns of their sexual unions, Lambert Strether confronts a situation which is comparatively static and by the exercise of his revitalized imagination comes eventually to a sympathetic understanding of it and more importantly to an understanding of himself. But Strether's growing awareness of the real situation obtaining between Chad and Madame de Vionnet and the minor crises occasioned by his periodic need to jettison responses to imagined situations, constitute only one side of the novel's development. As a guarantee of Strether's genuine involvement in the action, James also subjects his hero to the actual pressures exerted by Mrs Newsome, Madame de Vionnet and, to a lesser extent, Maria Gostrey. At every stage of his experience he must be made to feel for himself the conflicting pulls of duty, empathy and ease, represented to him by these three women. He is, at the same time, reflector, compositional centre and subject, combining in his person the functions of a Roland Mallet, Maisie Farange and an Isabel Archer; his illuminated consciousness serving as both tenor and vehicle for James's story, everything contributing to or flowing from his fine perceptions.

The culmination of events in the first half of the book, and the occasion that works for maximum effect is that of Gloriani's garden-party. In the preliminary statement for *The Ambassadors* he says: 'I "do" the occasion and the picture, evoke the place and influences, multiply so far as may be, the different sources of impression for our poor fermenting friend – the persons, figures, the strangenesses, nullities there present; with, above all, the wonderful intensity, oddity, amenity of the general intellectual, colloquial air.' Of course the anecdote about W. D. Howells which originally set the novel in motion attaches to this scene, and James is at pains in his sketch of the novel to show his ability to evoke the place and influence:

> He had found himself, one Sunday afternoon, with various other people, in the charming old garden attached to the house of a friend (also a friend of mine) in a particularly old-fashioned and pleasantly quiet part of the town; the garden that, with two or three others of the same sort near it, I myself knew, so that I could easily focus the setting. The old houses of the Faubourg St-Germain close round their gardens and shut them in, so that you don't see them from the street – only overlook them from all sorts of picturesque excrescences in the rear. I had a marked recollection of one of these wondrous concealed corners in especial, which was contiguous to the one mentioned by my friend: I used to know, many years ago, an ancient lady, long since dead, who lived in the house to which it belonged and whom, also on Sunday afternoons, I used to go to see. On one side of that one was another, visible from my old lady's windows, which was attached to a great convent of which I have forgotten the name, and which I think was one of the places of training for young missionary priests, whom we used to look down on, as they strode, always with a book in hand, in the straight alleys. It endeared to me, I recall, the house in question – the one where I used to call – that Madame Récamier had finally lived and died in an appartment of the *rez-de-chaussée*: but my ancient friend had known her and waited on her last days; and that the latter gave me a strange and touching image of her as she lay there dying, blind, and bereft of Chateaubriand, who was already dead. But I mention these slightly irrelevant things only to show that I *saw* the scene of my young friend's anecdote. (*Notebooks*, 372–3)

He then goes on to recount W. D. Howells's lament which is substantially reproduced in Strether's conversation with Little Bilham. Practising as he must, a strict economy, James has only limited opportunities to evoke for Strether the atmosphere of this over-poweringly rich civilization. His developed sense of structure would hardly allow him to send his hero off on a tour of Europe after the fashion of Christopher Newman while the essential action is suspended; yet Strether's sense of the accumulations of civilization must be presented as the strongest pull of all. To this end James creates a dense, heavily textured prose in which metaphor, rich imagery, and the breadth of literary, artistic, and historical reference, represent Strether's acute perceptions of the life to which he is being initiated. There are, in addition, three or four occasions when James can evoke Paris more fully and directly in scenes which take place at Notre Dame, the Louvre, the Luxembourg Gardens, and in

Madame de Vionnet's salon in the rue de Bellechasse. Of these Gloriani's garden-party offers him easily the most in the way of treatable surface.

In the previous two parts (III and IV) Strether, aided by the minor agents of his enlightenment, Waymarsh, Maria, and Little Bilham, had speculated exhaustively about the nature and degree of Chad's attachment. He has continued to speculate during his first meeting with Chad at the opera where they sit together mute through the 'long tension of the act', subservient to the 'imposed tribute to propriety', one of the ironic accidents, James insists, of a high civilization. But neither here nor later, when the two men actually discuss the subject, does Strether succeed in doing more than imagine all the frightening possibilities of Chad's life. As Maria Gostrey says at the end of Book IV:

> 'Everything's possible. We must see.'
> 'See?' he echoed with a groan. 'Haven't we seen enough?'
> 'I haven't,' she smiled.
> 'But do you suppose that Little Bilham has lied?'
> 'You must find out.'
> It made him almost turn pale. 'Find out any more?'
> He had dropped on a sofa for dismay; but she seemed, as she stood over him, to have the last word. 'Wasn't what you came out for to find out all?'
> (I, 166)

The dislocated structure of her last sentence hints at a revelation, of which the most emphatic quality will be its completeness, and their conversation also prepares us for the fact that guesswork is about to give way to spectacle. James prepares towards his great scene with confident deliberation.

In the event, such illumination as there is at the garden-party serves rather to dazzle Strether than to throw any real light on to Chad's affairs. The dialectical development of the novel gives way here to impressionism, as Strether is seen reacting to one after another of the elements which make up for him the momentous afternoon. There is first of course the garden itself which, elegant, sequestered, and hard of access, speaks to Strether, with its surrounding grave hotels of 'survival. transmission, association, a strong, indifferent, persistent order'. Its very unexpectedness strikes him more than anything yet with 'the note of the range of the immeasurable town' and sweeps away his usual landmarks and terms. His disorientation is confirmed by an encounter with his host Gloriani, which, though superficially just an exchange of friendly greetings, assumes for Strether in his keyed-up state, the nature of a trial:

He was to see again, repeatedly in remembrance, the medal-like Italian face, in which every line was an artist's own, in which time told only as tone and consecration; and he was to recall in especial, as the penetrating radiance, as the communication of the illustrious spirit itself, the manner in which, while they stood briefly, in welcome and response, face to face, he was held by the sculptor's eyes. He was not soon to forget them, all unconscious, unintending, preoccupied though they were, as the source of the deepest intellectual sounding to which he had ever been exposed. (I, 172)

Finally Strether takes part in a conversation with Little Bilham and Mrs Barrace which does nothing to restore him to his lost bearings. As his friends ironically described the high moral temper of Waymarsh, unbending in its stiff opposition to everything Paris stands for, ('he is like the Indian chief one reads about, who, when he comes up to Washington to see the Great Father, stands, wrapped in his blanket and gives no sign.') Strether muses sadly and seriously upon his own divided state; unable to wrap himself round with a protective attitude like Waymarsh, he is yet incapable of submitting himself completely to the bewildering fluidity of Paris. The scene ends with his querulous criticism of a society where appearances offer so little in the way of clues to what lies beneath.

All this is leading up to Strether's culminating peroration about life, in which his mounting sense of exclusion and attraction towards European civilization is finally articulated. Before he is allowed to deliver it, though, he is at last introduced to Madame de Vionnet. James is quite explicit in his notes to the novel about the way he wanted to treat this first meeting, but by the time he came to write the scene he had evidently undergone a change of mind. He originally intended her to strike Strether 'as a kind of person he had absolutely never seen, nor ever, with any distinctness, dreamed of', but the impression she gives him when they at last come face to face in the novel is one of being very little different, in fact, from Mrs Newsome or Mrs Pocock: 'why, accordingly, be in a flutter – Strether could even put it that way – about the unfamiliar phenomenon of the *femme-du-monde*? On these terms Mrs Newsome herself was as much of one.' Strether's inadequate appraisal of Marie de Vionnet and his consequent assumption imparted later to Maria Gostrey, that Chad's interest must be in Jeanne, her daughter, and not in Madame de Vionnet herself, lends a slight irony to his imperative speech celebrating the need to 'live' at all costs. As James first planned the episode, Strether's speech, based on an accurate guess about the real situation between Chad amd Madame de Vionnet, would have effectively represented his final insight about life and left little room for any further development. At one point, James obviously thought he could cover his tracks by not allowing Strether to speculate at all about the sense of mystification he experiences: 'this whole occasion puts so many new meanings into things, does its little part towards shifting so many landmarks and confounding so many small assumptions, that perhaps one case of ambiguity doesn't count more than another.' James's sense of artistic propriety rescued him from the minor discrepancies inherent in the original idea and he preserved the tight structure of the scene and of the whole, by having Strether respond only half-heartedly to Marie de Vionnet in an unsatisfactory meeting which is rendered more so by being quickly interrupted. In this way, his outburst to Little Bilham, while still being of great thematic importance, yet retains something of the provisional about it. The other possible solution to this minor difficulty would have been to delay Strether's meeting with Madame de Vionnet until after his speech to Little Bilham, but this would have had the effect of separating completely Strether's early development with its culmination in this speech, from his impression of Madame de Vionnet. From both the structural and the psychological point of view this would have been undesirable. The method he adopts allows him to create a tangible link between the two halves of the novel.

The strength of such a link depends upon establishing Madame de Vionnet as the new agent in Strether's growth and James devotes the next two books to this realization. Of course he does not neglect to keep his plot in play, and Strether continues his investigative process, but the primary effect of books VI and VII is to reveal Madame de Vionnet not so much scenically as pictorially as Strether's initial impressions of her are heavily overlaid by others. An examination of the techniques used in this section of the novel will perhaps throw some light on to the frequently expressed idea that James, in his later work, sacrificed texture to structure in his neglect of the particularity in which the art of fiction should be rooted. Edith Wharton, herself a novelist whose acute awareness of the world of appearances well fitted her to make the criticism, was one of the first to acuse James of allowing his characters to react together in a virtual vacuum:

> His latest novels, for all their profound moral beauty, seem to me more and more lacking in atmosphere, more and more severed from that thick nourishing human air in which we all live and move. The characters in *The Wings of the Dove* and *The Golden Bowl* seem isolated in a Crookes tube for our inspection: his stage was cleared like that of the *Théâtre Français* in the good old days when no chair or table was introduced that was not *relevant to the action* (a good rule for the stage, but an unnecessary embarrassment to fiction). Preoccupied by this, I one day said to him: 'What was your idea of suspending the four principal characters in *The Golden Bowl* in the void? What sort of life did they lead when they were not watching each other, and fencing with each other? Why have you stripped them of all the *human fringes* we necessarily trail after us through life?'

He looked at me in surprise, and I saw at once that the surprise was painful, and wished I had not spoken. I had assumed that his system was a deliberate one, carefully thought out, and had been genuinely anxious to hear his reasons. But after a pause of reflection he answered in a disturbed voice: 'My dear – I didn't know I had!' And I saw that my question, instead of starting one of our absorbing literary discussions, had only turned his startled attention of a peculiarity of which he had been completely unconscious.[9]

It is true that James nowhere in his work manifests much ability to render the detailed appearance as unmediated reality. His creative exuberance was always made to subserve the demands of a truly penetrating intelligence, and his love of formal economy led him to despise the achievements of those dedicated to the creation of a 'paradise of loose ends'; even Tolstoy's genius couldn't reconcile James to the kind of novel he called 'loose and baggy monsters'. Within the limits imposed by the demands of structure though, his own fiction exhibits a growing concern for, and an increasing inventiveness in the use of all kinds of texture.

In the first of the passages under discussion, Strether's sympathetic scrutiny of Madame de Vionnet's drawing-room is undertaken in the hope of inferring something of the essence of his hostess's character. As he takes her milieu 'all tenderly into account', contrasting her possessions with the collection of *objets d'art* in Chad's lovely home and Maria's 'little museum of bargains', he discovers something different in the peace, dignity, and stability which wrap Madame de Vionnet around. The books, harps, urns and medallions from the time of Madame de Stael and Chateaubriand lead him to guess at 'intense little preferences and sharp little exclusions, a deep suspicion of the vulgar and a personal view of the right.' The swords and medals he is sure occupy the surrounding glass cases symbolize for him the private honour and the air of supreme respectability which pervade the house and strike the strongest note of its moral furniture. Of course it *is* the moral furniture that interests Strether, and when he comes across a copy of the *Revue*, with its slightly incongruous modernity, he is led to suspect Chad's interested influence. Their ensuing conversation pursues this subject. Analysis of the technique which depends upon a multitude of accumulated connotations and reverberations, as well as upon sudden, abrupt shifts in meaning, can only simplify the captured subtleties. A short quotation, will, however, show the technique working. Everything in this concluding paragraph confirms the interpreted description preceding it, and the last, significant sentence throws them forward into their first major conversational battle:

9. *A Backward Glance* (New York, 1934).

> She was seated, near the fire, on a small stuffed and fringed chair, one of the few modern articles in the room; and she leaned back in it with her hands clasped in her lap and no movement, in all her person, but the fine, prompt play of her deep young face. The fire, under the low white marble, undraped and academic, had burnt down to the silver ashes of light wood; one of the windows, at a distance, had opened to the mildness and stillness, out of which, in the short pauses, came the faint sound, pleasant and homely, almost rustic, of a plash and a clatter of *sabots* from some coach-house on the other side of the court. Mme de Vionnet, while Strether sat there, was not to shift her posture by an inch. (I, 216–17)

Strether soon meets Madame de Vionnet again at Chad's dinner-party where he is struck again by the Cleopatra-like variety of her manifestations. All his categories, psychological, social, and moral, are surprised by her multifold genius, and this amazement is reflected in his awed, romantic description of her as some mythological beauty from the sea. James, speaking of the need, in this section of the novel, to 'do' the developing contact between Madame de Vionnet and Strether, admits that she is a subject which offers him too great a wealth for his comfort. He avoids the danger of having his heroine take control of the development by making her conform rigidly to her function as catalyst to that process which is taking place in Strether, and which is 'of the core of the subject . . .. Singularly, admirably Mme de Vionnet comes after a little to stand, with Strether, for most of the things that make the *charm* of civilization as he now revives it and imaginatively reconstructs, morally reconsiders, so to speak, civilization.' It may be objected that James goes too far in stressing her representative function and loses through it altogether her common humanity. In fact, each of these carefully drawn pictures is the prelude to a conversation between the two, in which James establishes beyond question her individual psychology.

The third and last of these occasions takes place in Notre Dame. Under the spell of the mighty monument, Strether muses with 'vague tenderness' about one of the unkown figures inhabiting the church:

> She reminded our friend – since it was the way of nine-tenths of his current impressions to act as recalls of things imagined – of some fine, firm, concentrated heroine of an old story, something he had heard, read, something that, having had a hand for drama, he might himself have written, renewing her courage, renewing her clearness, in splendidly protected mediation. (II, 6)

It is, of course, Madame de Vionnet, and his discovery leads him once more to ponder the implications of such a phenomenon. Above all, her appearance there testifies to the unassailable innocence of her relations with Chad, Strether concludes. She would never, he decided, come there to flaunt an insolence of sexual guilt. The pattern of this scene is almost indentical with the earlier one in Madame de Vionnet's salon. Strether offers her lunch at a restaurant, and here they embark again on one of their eager, probing discussions about Chad. Again picture is linked to dialogue by a short passage similar to the one quoted above in which the 'quiet, soft acuteness' of her mind is foreshadowed in the play of her grey eyes.

James's subtle control of his theme through the manipulation of picture and scene make such criticisms as Edith Wharton's seem clumsily irrelevant. The comparatively crude, mechanical interaction of character and environment in *The House of Mirth* and *The Custom of the Country*, sufficiently indicate by contrast the limitations of the realistic novel of manners.

James had originally hoped to keep his novel down to ten parts of ten thousand words each. By compressing and foreshortening the material in the next three books and by cutting out much of the pleasant but seemingly casual comedy engendered by the irruption of the Pococks, James could easily have done so. That he didn't suggests he counted on them for more than was apparent in his stated intention to produce entertainment and interest by the creation of 'sharp types'. Elsewhere in his preliminary statement he suggests the possibility of more important function: 'Contrast and opposition is naturally here played straight up. The Vionnets and the Pococks, Chad and his sister, Pocock and his brother-in-law, Chad and Pocock's sister, Strether and Pocock, Pocock and Strether, Strether and everyone and everything, but Strether and Mrs Pocock in especial, with everything brought to a head by *her* — there is no lack of stuff.' Here too, there is a suggestion of the light way in which he will treat these oppositions, and the mood throughout is one of muted comedy.

Despite some excellent scenes in these three books, including the first one in Sarah's salon and that in which Mamie Pocock's brooding consciousness is dramatized in Strether's sympathetic projection; and despite the fact that James contrives to develop the novel's main action with Marie de Vionnet's announcement of Jeanne's engagement, while at the same time building up a new comic character in Jim Pocock, there is yet a sense in which there *is* a lack of stuff in this part of the book. James was faced with the problem of bringing in Sarah Pocock, giving her time to assess the whole situation, work on Chad as best she can, and finally break with Strether. Had he foreshortened his perspectives any further he might have seriously weakened its proper development, as he was conscious of having done in the central section of *Roderick Hudson*. His solution to the problem was to pack as much as possible between Sarah's arrival in

Paris and her final break with Strether. James makes every small part function in the whole, even here. Jim's comic 'awfulness' is a calculated feature of Chad's possible response to the appeal of Woollett; Maria's conversation with Strether is used to wring all the meaning out of the decision to marry off Jeanne; and the brittle comedy of Sarah's first meeting with Madame de Vionnet strengthens Strether's sense of the values the two women symbolize. Nevertheless, the need to introduce and keep in play the development of three new characters inevitably leads to something of a drop after the concentrated focus of the preceding chapters. Even that episode, which, by virtue of its compositional novelty, is specifically designed to give a lift to the action, impresses one more as a peripheral *tour de force* than as a major representational obstacle overcome. Strether's reconstruction of the events in Mamie Pocock's mind and the description of their tacit sympathetic communion on the balcony of the Paris hotel, transposed into an extended simile, reads like a casual essay in a technique that was only to attain its full expression in *The Golden Bowl* and *The Ivory Tower*.

Reading through the various conversational encounters which make up this part of the novel, it is hard to resist the conclusion that the chief purpose they serve is to allow one to feel, through the various reactions of Strether, Chad, Maria, Waymarsh, Mlle Barrace, Madame de Vionnet, Little Bilham, and even Jim and Mamie, the long reach of Sarah Pocock's continuous, massive indignation during the three weeks prior to her interview with Strether. In any event she is certainly the chief subject of discussion in every conversation but one, and when she and Strether finally do come face to face to effect the final rupture, the ground for their meeting has been well enough prepared. James, of course, is careful to make the reason for their actual breach the critical locus of the novel's final developments:

'You don't, on your honour, appreciate Chad's fortunate development?'
'Fortunate?' she echoed again. And indeed she was prepared. 'I call it hideous.'
'Her departure had been for some minutes marked as imminent, and she was already at the door that stood open to the court, from the threshold of which she delivered herself of this judgement. It rang out so loud as to produce for the first time the hush of everything else. Strether quite, as an effect of it, breathed less bravely; he could acknowledge it, but simply enough.
'Oh, if you think that – !'
'Then all is at an end? So much the better. I do think that!' (II, 183)

Thus the way is prepared for Strether's ultimate test. Freed from narrower contingencies and having forfeited 'the confidence, the esteem, the affection of a noble woman, the good opinion, frankly, of a noble community; and at any rate the promise of ease and security, a refined, and even a luxurious, home for the rest of his days', he is brought within sight of what James calls 'the crux of his case'.

Despite his earlier claim that *The Ambassadors* caused him no 'moment of subjective intermittence, never one of those alarms as for a suspected hollow beneath one's feet', James admitted in another part of the Preface that this novel, like all his others, suffers from his constant difficulty in executing an original plan:

> One would like, at such an hour as this, for critical license, to go into the matter of the noted inevitable deviation (from too fond an original vision) that the exquisite treachery even of the straightest execution may ever be trusted to inflict even on the most mature plan – the case being that, though one's last reconsidered production always seems to bristle with that particular evidence, *The Ambassadors*, would place a flood of such light at my service.

Denying himself such revelations he goes on to discuss his use of presentational methods other than the scenic, and as illustration of his point mentions Strether's first meeting with Chad at the opera where he achieves 'expressional decency' under another law. This recollection brings him back again to a general point and he concludes:

> The true inwardness of this may be at bottom but that one of the suffered treacheries has consisted precisely, for Chad's whole figure and presence, of a direct presentability diminished and compromised – despoiled, that is, of its *proportional* advantage; so that, in a word, the whole economy of his author's relation to him has at important points to be re-determined.

Disagreement and dissatisfaction among critics concerning the last part of *The Ambassadors* and particularly about Chad's final development may testify to an ambiguity in the character deriving not so much from an inconsistent conception as from James's attempt to solve certain difficulties of presentation. That he did encounter such problems in the ending of the novel may reasonably be inferred from the fact of his having considerably amended his initial scheme. For the most part, the outline in the Notebooks is a surprisingly accurate guide to his actual practice in the novel; Part XII is the only major deviation.

When Chad agrees to remain in Paris a little longer at Strether's request, it is because, as Strether remarks to Maria Gostrey, he already half wants to. We are denied direct access to Chad's motives, and to some critics the neat reversal of roles and Chad's subsequent submission to Strether's will imply an unwarranted sacrifice of character to narrative pattern. In point of fact, Chad does explain himself, not at this point, but in the last conversation the two men have before the discovery scene:

'It was six weeks ago that I thought I had come out.'
Strether took it well in. 'But you hadn't come out?'
'I don't know – it's what I *want* to know. And if I could have sufficiently wanted – by myself – to go back, I think I might have found out.' (II, 215–16)

It is not difficult to see why James thought of this last scene between the sacrificed and the saved as being potentially the most beautiful and interesting morsel in the book. As a solution to the structural and psychological problems he was faced with, though, his projected ending is mechanical and unreal. The method of the novel whereby Strether reduces everyone else to subjection always runs a risk of reducing the minor characters even further; relegating them, in fact, to puppet-like projections of the hero's over-active imagination. In avoiding that temptation here, Chad necessarily has to undergo something of a transformation, and with it the novel's main thesis is to some extent undermined. Throughout his entire experience Strether's case against Woollett has rested upon what he calls Chad's 'fortunate development'. His faith in the beneficial effect of European civilization in general and Madame de Vionnet in particular, in teaching Chad how to live, holds through every vicissitude. Even as late as on one of his last visits to Chad at his home in the Boulevard Malesherbes, he continues to reflect on this approved facility in his friend. In Part XII though, James begins to suggest that Chad may not have been changed in any radical or permanent way after all. Strether perceives as much in deducing the cause of Madame de Vionnet's fear:

What was at bottom the matter with her, embroider as she might and disclaim as she might – what was at bottom the matter with her was simply Chad himself. It was of Chad she was, after all, renewedly afraid; the strange strength of her passion was the very strength of her fear; she clung to *him*, Lambert Strether, as to a source of safety she had tested, and, generous, graceful, truthful as she might try to be, exquisite as she was, she dreaded the term of his being within reach. With the sharpest perception yet, it was like a chill in the air to him, it was almost appalling, that a creature so fine could be, by mysterious forces, a creature so exploited. For, at the end of all things, they *were* mysterious: she had but made Chad what he was – so why could she think she had made him infinite? She had made him better, she made him best, she had made him anything one would; but it came to our friend with supreme queerness that he was none the less only Chad. (II, 254–5)

Later, Chad himself will speak of his developing interest in the advertising business, and the suggestion will even be made that he might also have another mistress in London. Whatever James might mean by 'knowing how to live', such knowledge could hardly be attributed to Chad Newsome as he is shown in the final chapters of

The Ambassadors; his coarse materialism and blunted sensibility conform more readily to the idea of him expressed earlier by Sarah Pocock. It is possible to interpret the transformation in various ways. Oscar Cargill writes about Strether's 'complete disillusionment' with Chad, and Stephen Spender interprets it as proof that it is Strether who has 'lived' and not Chad. James himself speaks of the strange irony of Madame de Vionnet having moulded Chad into what he essentially is: a restless philanderer. But none of these explanations is really satisfactory; they all ignore James's failure to reconcile a discrepancy between the final development of the plot and the general pattern of values established by the rest of the novel. The origin of this discrepancy can be traced to the influence on James of the *pièce bien faite* with its subordination of consistent characterization to the demands of an inflexible plot structure. Steven Stanton has enumerated the obligatory features of the Well-Made Play as written by Scribe, Augier and Sardou:

(1) A plot based on a secret known to the audience but withheld from certain characters (who have long been engaged in a battle of wits) until its revelation (or the direct consequence thereof) in the climactic scene serves to unmask a fraudulent character and restore to good fortune the suffering hero, with whom the audience has been made to sympathize; (2) a pattern of increasingly intense action and suspense, prepared by exposition (this pattern assisted by contrived entrances and exits, letters and other devices); (3) a series of ups and downs in the hero's fortunes, caused by his conflict with an adversary; (4) the counterpunch of peripeteia and *scène à faire*, marking, respectively, the lowest and the highest point in the hero's adventures, and brought about by the disclosure of secrets to the opposing side; (5) a central misunderstanding or *quid pro quo* made obvious to the spectator but withheld from the participants; (6) a logical and credible dénouement; and (7) the reproduction of the overall action pattern in the individual acts.[10]

Whilst the relevance of this formula, or parts of it, to *The Ambassadors* is fairly obvious, it is no less obvious that James, like Ibsen and Shaw who were also influenced by nineteenth-century French drama, far transcends the formal limits of his models. Scribe wrote nearly four hundred plays without creating a memorable character, and Sardou, writing in his Preface to *La Haine*, describes a method of compostion patently inimical to the development of solid personalities. Like a detective-story writer he first composed his *scène à faire* and then worked backwards from this to fill in the rest of the plot.

James, on the other hand, in a letter written about the time he was working on *The Ambassadors*, criticizing the behaviour of a character

10. Introduction to *Camille and other Plays* (New York, 1957).

in Paul Bourget's *La Duchesse Bleue* for the same faults which mar the work of Scribe and Sardou, demonstrates a much more sophisticated concept of fictional character:

> I think I see, myself, positively what he would have done; and in general he is, to my imagination as you give him, too much in character, too little mysterious. So is Mme de Bonnivet – so too even, is the actress. Your love of intellectual daylight, absolutely your love of complexities, is an injury to the patches of ambiguity and the abysses of shadow which really are the clothing – or much of it – of the effects that constitute the material of our trade.[11]

James's failure to reconcile the mysteries of Chad's character, the abysses of shadow necessary as a guarantee of his vitality, with the demands of a symmetrical, intellectually complex structure, is the one major flaw in *The Ambassadors*.

I earlier put forward, in opposition to Quentin Anderson's thesis, a view of James which sees him in the late novels as a descendant of Emerson, Hawthorne and Thoreau, rather than as his father's direct disciple. Anderson is so busy charting the parallels between the art of the son and the father's philosophy that he completely ignores the implications for criticism of the relationship. I believe him to be quite wrong in his reading of *The Ambassadors*, but much nearer the mark in his analysis of *The Wings of The Dove* and *The Golden Bowl*, even if his approach to them is equally suspect. The importance of this, though, can be made clearer when we see the novels as a belated expression of what I discussed earlier as 'the voice of Hope.' Its elevation into a philosophical allegory serves only to obscure for the reader the origin of the truths James thought he had established. It is James himself who points out in *The American Scene* how often he had occasion to turn to Emerson finding in him 'a sense of moving in large intellectual space'. He goes on to praise Emerson's genius 'which has made him so, for the attentive peoples, the first, and the only really rare American spirit in letters.' There should be no need to labour this point. The relationship between James and his New England predecessors is a well attested fact. It accounts for much that is good in James's novels as well as for that which is sentimental, romatic, and provincial in the worst sense. It is at best an indirect relationship working to the surface of the novels usually in the form of what Emerson himself called the 'optative mood'. There is, I want to say, in James's presentation of Milly Theale an idealism that is finally naïve and unjustifiable. James envisages her as a princess, 'the

11. Letter to Paul Bourget (See note 2, Chapter 2).

heir of all the ages' – F. O. Mathiessen as 'the most resonant symbol for what he had to say about humanity',[12] and Quentin Anderson simply as 'divine love'. I think it would help towards a truer appreciation of her fictional quality if we were to substitute for these views one which sees her as a late representative of New England idealism, not unlike the type envisaged by Emerson:

> But all these of whom I speak are not proficients; they are novices; they only show the road on which man should travel, when the soul has greater health and prowess. Yet let them feel the dignity of their charge, and deserve the larger power. Their heart is the ark in which the fire is concealed which shall burn in a broader and universal flame. Let them obey the Genius then most when his impulse is wildest; then most when he seems to lead to uninhabitable deserts of thought and life; for the path which the hero travels alone is the highway of health and of benefit to mankind . . . the thoughts which these few hermits strove to proclaim by silence, as well as by speech, not only by what they did, but by what they forebore to do, shall abide in beauty and strength, to reorganize themselves in nature, to invest themselves anew in other, perhaps a higher endowed and happier mixed clay than ours, in fuller union with the surrounding system.[13]

On the other hand, Marius Bewley in *The Complex Fate* shows how more specific influences in Hawthorn were at work in the creation of Milly Theale, how the dove image may have been derived from Hilda in *The Marble Faun*, and how a summing up of the traits held in common by these 'angels' conclusively shows how near James draws to his predecessor, 'expecially to some of his predecessors' sorriest aspects.' Before proceeding to a discussion of how far James fell short in his presentation of Milly as an emblem it is important to follow up her development in the novel's action for our assent to the values offered symbolically must depend also on the degree to which they are concretely realized in terms of particular human personalities.

'The idea', James tells us in his Preface, 'reduced to its essence, is that of a young person conscious of a great capacity for life, but early stricken and doomed, condemned to die under short respite, while also enamoured of the world; aware moreover of the condemnation and passionately desiring to "put in" before extinction as many of the finer vibrations as possible, and so achieve, however briefly and brokenly, the sense of having lived.' To give her liberty, choice and appreciation, she must be: 'possessed of all things, all but the single most precious assurance; freedom and money and a mobile mind and personal charm, the power to interest and attach . . . she should be the last fine flower, blooming alone, for the fullest attestation of her

12. *Henry James: The Major Phase* (New York, 1963).
13. *Miscellanies.*

freedom, of an "old" New York stem . . . the heir of all the ages, balked of her inheritance'. She is to form the centre, a vessel of sensibility, fine enough to register every meaning converging in upon her from a circumference which should be 'every bit as treatable'. In pursuit of this ideal he resorts to what he calls a 'merciful indirection, all as if to approach her circuitously, deal with her at second hand, as an unspotted princess is ever dealt with.' Consequently he begins from 'far back' with the situation into which Milly will be precipitated. It is a situation which allows James to make the most of the Dove's descent and exposure. Edwardian society is presented in terms of the brilliant possibilities for life, a largeness of style which provides Milly with just the element she can operate in, and which is calculated to elicit from her 'all the freshness of response of her young life, the freshness of the first and only prime.' Largeness of style requires, however, the liberating factor of a correspondingly large bank balance; and a vivid rendering of the economic pressures which have driven Kate Croy to accept her rich Aunt Maud's hospitality take us behind the smooth, stylish exterior with which Milly is to be later confronted. Kate is in love with Merton Densher, a poor journalist, and they carry on a clandestine relationship and hope that somehow they will be able to 'square' Aunt Maud, who has set her heart on a 'good' marriage for Kate. Their opportunity comes when Kate conceives a design for the appropriation of Milly's fortune. The scheme is characterized by Kate's 'hideous intelligence' and high style: 'it had really, her sketch of the affair, a high colour and a great style, at all of which he gazed a minute as at a picture by a master.' Beneath the preserved appearances, though, we can glimpse the depths of moral ugliness associated with 'the world'. Densher is to marry Milly, who is already half in love with him, in the knowledge that she must soon die and leave her fortune to him. The plan is put into operation but finally frustrated. Milly in her role as 'divine love' displays her 'good faith' and her imagination, nevertheless, by putting in Densher's hand the power to save himself. She does leave him a fortune and it is the measure of her power that he has come to the point where he can no longer go through with the plan. He offers to reject the money and marry Kate 'as we were'. But she declines the offer with what is a final tribute to Milly: 'We shall never be again as we were.'

Those who would say most for *The Wings of The Dove* are well represented by Dorothea Krook, who calls it James's *Antony and Cleopatra*, 'his supreme testament to the beauty of the world and the greatness of the human spirit taken to the furthest limits of their power and glory.'[14] It is in most respects an unfortunate comparison.

14. *'The Wings of the Dove'* (*The Cambridge Journal*, Vol. VII, 1953).

In an effort to give his optimistic idealism its fullest and finest expression James has strained the limits to which it can be taken, and the elements of 'fire' and 'air' in which Milly has her being prove altogether too thin a medium even to sustain the rarefied life of a 'vibrating' consciousness such as Milly's. She also elicits from critics the inevitable comparison with Minny Temple, James's cousin, on whom he is said to have consciously modelled her, Minny's ghost, in his own words, 'wrapped in the dignity and the beauty of art . . . silvered over and set apart.' In abstracting the qualities he so admired in his cousin, 'a sense for verity of character and the play of life in others – a taste for life as life, as personal living', and reinvesting them in Milly Theale he necessarily dissevers the symbolic content from the warm, human attributes of Isabel Archer whom we remember:

> with her meagre knowledge, her inflated ideals, her confidence at once innocent and dogmatic, her temper at once exacting and indulgent, her mixture of curiosity and fastidiousness, of vivacity and indifference, her desire to look very well and to be if possible, even better, her determination to see, to try, to know, her combination of the delicate, desultory, flame-like spirit and the eager and personal creature of conditions . . . would be an easy target for scientific criticism. (53)

He has also to sacrifice the acute critical observation of detail with which he could bring to life another American girl, Verena Tarrant. Milly Theale's background is sketched with a vagueness which adds to the romantic flavour, commensurate with her later triumphs:

> It was a New York history, confused as yet, but multitudinous, of the loss of parents, brothers, sisters, almost every human appendage, all on a scale and with a sweep that had required the greater stage; it was a New York legend of affecting, of romantic isolation, and beyond everything, it was by most accounts, in respect to the mass of money so piled on the girl's back, a set of New York possibilities . . . . This was poetry – it was also history, Mrs Stringham thought, to a finer tune than even Maeterlinck and Pater, than Marbot and Gregorovius. (I, 95–100)

Her mission is to take possession in a symbolic, spiritual manner, of the world, just as, in another way the Ververs take possession of the world in *The Golden Bowl*. Her development is towards an apotheosis, of which she herself is only too aware. At the moment of one of her greatest triumphs when she is most in the world and on the point of being compared with the portrait of an Italian princess she becomes aware of the 'beauty and the history and the facility and the splendid midsummer glow; it was a sort of manificent maximum, a pink dawn of an apotheosis.' Her real truimph consists, though, in Densher's redemption, and it is presented exclusively through his consciousness. Throughout the novel he resists the suggestion that he is in love with her maintaining that he didn't even feel curious about her; but as her 'trust' and 'inscrutable mercy' work on him he comes to feel that 'something had happened to him, too beautiful and too sacred to describe. He had been to his recovered sense forgiven, dedicated, blessed.'

If it is true that the greatest instrument of moral good is the imagination then Milly Theale's insights leading to her final magnanimous act may appear indicative of a fine and civilized nature. Wrapped about as they are, however, with her self-conscious piety, her immutable sentimentality, and James's romantic imagery, they cannot fail to lack the real spontaneity we should associate with her. Not only to Susan Stringham does Milly's Veronese palace seem 'one of the courts of Heaven, the court of a reigning seraph, a sort of vice-queen of an angel', but Milly herself obviously finds satisfaction in the idea of such an omniscient role:

> The Romance for her, yet once more, would be to sit there for ever, through all her time, as in a fortress; and the idea became an image of never going down, of remaining aloft in the divine dustless air, where she would hear but the plash of the water against stone. (II, 133)

The ostensible justification for her 'excluded, disinherited state', is her disease and imminent death, but in reality such a factor as this was the necessary condition for her to live at all. To some extent a similar argument can be made against Lambert Strether, whose age absolves him from the dangers of total submission to experience, and of the three late protagonists it is only Maggie Verver who really takes 'full in the face, the whole assault of life' and who comes through without figuratively turning her face to the wall.

There can be little doubt that James intended *The Golden Bowl* to represent 'the eventual divine consensus behind all the small comedies and tragedies of the international', and in so far as it does this the novel is very rich in accumulated shades of meaning. Indeed it has proved too rich for most of its readers, who have disagreed with each other on almost every possible point of interpretation in regard both to James's intention and to his achieved effects. Without pursuing these disagreements very far it is possible to see in them an indication of *The Golden Bowl's* central ambiguity; of the equivocations never quite resolved, and of the novel's anomalous position in James's canon. A classical simplicity of structure and a perfectly symmetrical development allow for the complexities I have mentioned to be introduced by way of symbol, imagery, and the involved, tortuous monologues of the principal characters. These, the four main actors, all have a considerable history in the growth of James's international theme; especially Adam Verver and his daughter Maggie. We have met before Mr Leavenworth, Christopher

Newman and Mr Bender, the fabulously rich American connoisseur who has made his millions in an unspecified manner before retiring to pursue a different kind of acquisition. His daughter is also a familiar figure – one of the long line of Jamesian heroines endowed like all her predecessor, but in a high degree, with money, intelligence and innocence. The representatives of Europe are Prince Amerigo – 'A Roman and a real galantuomo' and Charlotte Stant – expatriate American, herself 'a rare, special product'. They are both brilliant, beautiful polyglots, with an instinctive mastery of the 'forms' of living, a social capital which is their compensation for their lack of any other. This lack of money has led them to break off a love affair which extends back before the beginning of the novel's action, and the Prince at the beginning of the book becomes engaged to Maggie Verver. James is quite explicit about all the reasons on every side for the marriage. For Mr Verver the Prince represents a part of his collection – 'a rarity, an object of beauty, an object of price, a *morceau de musée*; and Maggie herself admits that it was not the Prince's personal qualities which attracted her, but the generations behind him – 'The follies and the crimes, the plunder and the waste . . .. Where, therefore,' she had put it to him again, 'without your archives, annals, infamies, would you have been?' As for the Prince: 'What was this so important step he had just taken but the desire for some new history that should, so far as possible, contradict, and even if need be flatly dishonour the old? If what had come to him wouldn't do he must make something different. He perfectly recognized – always in his humility – that the material for the making had to be Mr Verver's millions.'

The wedding takes place and Maggie's thoughts now turn to her father, with whom she has been particularly intimate and whom she fears will now feel increasingly sad and lonely. She attempts in all innocence, knowing nothing of the Prince's love affair with Charlotte, to bring together her father and Charlotte, not only in the hope that a marriage between them would make reparation to him for the loss of his daughter but also in the belief that she will at the same time be doing a favour to her friend and also adding to her family a further element of greatness. This marriage also takes place eventually but the hoped-for consequences are not entailed. Maggie and her father renew their former intimacy and the Prince and Charlotte, thrown together again, resume their broken love affair. The first part of the novel ends with their expedition to Gloucester after a weekend house party and Maggie's first intimations of the real nature of the situation in which she is involved.

The second part of the novel, presented entirely through Maggie's consciousness, deals with her attempt to restore her marriage and with it her former happiness. She realizes that to do so she cannot afford to take 'the straight vindictive view, the rights of resentment, the rages of jealousy, the protests of passion.' For unless she takes it 'full in the face' she must inevitably 'give them up' and this was 'marvellously not to be thought of.' So while still preserving 'the serenities and dignities and decencies' she yet manages to effect a remarkable transformation in their relationships involving, however, the separation from her father, who takes Charlotte back with him to American City leaving the Prince and Maggie united by a bond of love and common knowledge of each other's intrinsic worth.

From this description of the novel's plot reduced to its bare factual outline no normative propositions concerning *The Golden Bowl's* implicit scheme of values could possibly be deduced. The fiercest controversy has usually raged around James's presentation of Maggie Verver's character, critics finding in her anything from 'divine love' to 'heartless Machiavellian absolutism'. It will be instructive to look first at James's presentation of Adam Verver, her father. I have said already that he follows on from a long line of American business men, but the crucial point is, does James intend us to see and react to the possible ironies in his presentation or are we to take him at his own estimate of himself? Maggie of course, sees him as a hero:

> With which, his glasses still fixed on her, his hands in his pockets, his hat pushed back, his legs a little apart, he seemed to plant or to square himself with the kind of assurance which had occurred to him he might as well treat her to, in default of other things, before they changed their subject. It had the effect for her of a reminder –a reminder of all he was, of all he had done, of all, above and beyond of his being her perfect little father, she might take him as representing, take him as having quite eminently, in the eyes of two hemispheres, been capable of, and as therefore wishing, not – was it? – illegitimately, to call her attention to. The 'successful' and beneficent person, the beautiful, bountiful original dauntlessly wilful great citizen, the consummate collector and infallible high authority he had been and still was – these things struck her on the spot as making up for him in a wonderful way a character she must take into account in dealing with him either for pity or for envy. (II, 240)

Her opinion is shared by Quentin Anderson, who thinks Verver represents both God and man – as Maggie is divine love so he is divine wisdom. Caroline Gordon maintains that Verver is James's arch creation with certain remarkable qualities, notably, 'he is innocent in the deepest sense of the word, but he has tremendous moral power' which he uses to subjugate Charlotte, 'the terrible woman of the future'.[15] On the other hand there are reminders of those other American millionaires whom James treated with such cool critical detachment in earlier books. In his inflated idealism he sees himself in the image of Keats's 'stout Cortez', as a great

15. See note 1.

beneficiary to American life, equal somehow to the 'great seers, the invokers and encouragers of beauty', an ancestor, as it were, of Rockefeller, who with his medieval abbey overlooking the Hudson was merely putting into effect Verver's plan to release his fellow Americans from the 'bondage of ugliness': 'surely, we are not to think of James as envisaging the wholesale abduction of European art and its monumental installation in a western American city as the "ideal programme" for retired tycoons devoting themselves to the charitable dispensation of culture! The idea is so at odds with one's sense of what James stood for that it is almost embarrassing to have to argue its absurdity.'[16]

It is indeed hard to reconcile any other view of Verver than the ironic with what James has given us of this type before, and Christophe Wegelin goes on to argue that the final separation of the father and daughter represents for Maggie the escape from American immaturity, enabling her finally to fulfil her potentialities. Though Adam Verver is not of the utmost importance these contradictory views of him do entail, for the people who hold them, different versions of the novel as a whole, differing significantly in the role allotted to the Americans. It is significant because it hints at the ambiguity in James's own approach to America which will become clearer when we discuss *The American Scene* and *The Ivory Tower*.

The major bone of contention among critics of *The Golden Bowl*, though, is Maggie's part in the novel and her symbolic value in the international situation. I have already cited the view of her as an embodiment of divine love, mastering the evils of European experience without losing her 'Edenique' inspiration when I summarized Quentin Anderson's thesis. Others in the same vein have seen Maggie as 'Beatrice – the Queen or at least the Princess of all forms of knowledge walking in human flesh',[17] or as a living embodiment of the Christian concept of Caritas. This is the common view expressed in its most exalted form and I do not want to discuss it here. A more unusual interpretation strongly urged by Joseph Firebaugh depends on an entirely different explanation of Maggie's character and actions.[18] Firebaugh very persuasively presents Maggie as a self-righteous absolutist manipulating life to suit her own Machiavellian purposes. He provides instances of her selfish cruelty and complacency when confronted with the suffering of the Prince and Charlotte, and even of her father. At the end of the novel she can speak of her own loss quite coldly and impersonally:

16. C. Wegelin, 'The Internationalism of *The Golden Bowl*' (Nineteenth Century Fiction, Vol. XI, 1956).
17. R. P. Blackmur. See note 4.
18. 'The Ververs' (*Essays in Criticism*, 1954).

'Oh yes,' Maggie quite lucidly declared, 'lost to each other really much more than Amerigo and Charlotte are; since for them it's just, it's right, it's deserved, while for us it's only sad and strange and not caused by our fault.' (II, 294)

Thus backed by wealth and intellect Maggie wields her authority in the interests of ownership and power and the preservation of a preconceived idea. Undeniably these elements do enter into James's presentation of Maggie but where Firebaugh goes astray is in suggesting that the interpretation he offers conforms exactly with James's own plan for the novel. He insists that *The Golden Bowl* is a 'gigantic horrified protest against the manouvring of appearances to favour *a priori* concepts of the good, true, and the beautiful; against the use of knowledge to preserve a specious appearance of innocence.' Thus it attacks the gentility of James's era and tells us that 'if our sympathies are to any extent with Charlotte and the Prince that is because James wanted them to be; if James made a mistake in a matter so basic to the novel as this, he is hardly the master his critics concede him to have been. If the general moral background of the book is offensive to readers as sensitive as Mr Leavis, that is because James wanted them to be offended by it.' An assumption of James's status as a master and the James family's dislike of self-righteousness are hardly sufficient evidence for Firebaugh's theory of *The Golden Bowl* as a planned protest 'against the crushing of human emotion by a harsh absolutist hand', and James's design for Maggie as a 'politico-economic monster' – a symbol of the 'cartalized, totalitarian State'.

On the contrary there can be little doubt that James envisaged a role for Maggie not unlike that enacted by Milly Theale. Like Milly she has to contend with 'the horror of finding evil seated all at its ease, where she had only dreamed of good.' To take this full in the face without any recoil and withdrawal is, for James, undoubtedly the sign that his heroine had at last come through. In the magnificent scene at Fawns where Maggie turns the tables on Charlotte, James shows that he is fully aware of the deceitful and cruel-seeming methods employed by Maggie. The justification being of course that all her manipulation serves a noble end; namely the promotion of Good. If we are to criticize James it must be for flaws in his moral system, not for the novel's construction, for the boundless good faith and optimism so deeply rooted that no experience can really penetrate to them. It has been noticed before that in these late novels James resorts to the language of the fairy story and essentially that is what *The Golden Bowl* is, a fairy story with some of its attendant sentimentality. The Europe of *The Golden Bowl* is little more than 'a lighted and decorated stage' prepared for the arrival of a morally superior Princess whose money is merely the prerequisite of that superiority. Her background is steadfastly ignored and this accounts for the implicit irony in Adam Verver's life – the flat incompatibility of his innocence with his millions.

In 1904 though, James returned to America to see for himself what was happening there and the result of that visit was the creation of Abel Gaw and a marked reorientation of his attitudes towards his native country. The American girl too came in for his scrutiny and she emerges as a very different creature from Maggie Verver:

> Falsely beguiled, pitilessly forsaken, thrust forth in ignorance and folly, what do I know, helpless chit as I can but be, about manners or tone, about proportion of perspective, about modesty or mystery, about a condition of things that involves, for the interest and the grace of life, other forms of existence than this poor little mine. How can I do all the grace, all the interest as I'm expected to? – yes, literally all the interest that isn't interest on the money. I'm expected to supply it all – while I wander and stray in the desert – haven't I – . . . been too long abandoned and to much betrayed? Isn't it too late, and am I not, don't you think, practically lost? (*The American Scene*, 431)

8

A felicity forever
gone

The American industrial revolution and the great entrepreneurs who were responsible, if not for its inception, then at least for its incredibly rapid development, are already matter for legend. In the thirty years or so which separate *The Europeans* from *The Ivory Tower*, the transformation of America was accomplished and the society James knew and wrote about in 1878 was indeed gone for ever. What had taken its place he was not really to discover until his return in 1904. It is true that he had dealt in his work with the American millionaire and the 'rape of Europe', but the naïvety of his conception of what such a figure as Christopher Newman would be like is easily demonstrated by the lives of such men as Frick, Vanderbilt and Jay Gould. These men and their contemporaries – Hill, Harriman, Rockfeller, Carnegie, Duke, Cornell and Morgan: a comparative handful of multi-millionaires – had brought into being an industrial power as remote and different in its own way from mid-century New England as they both were from the Europe James had come to know so well.

America's population in 1840 was in the region of 20 millions; by 1900 it had been supplemented by another 20 million European immigrants. There were by this date 17 million wage-earners, four and a half million of them engaged in manufacturing, and 40 per cent of the population were living in towns or cities. The railroads had expanded into a network of 200,000 miles necessitating the growth of such cities as Chicago – twenty times larger in 1910 than it had been fifty years before. Indeed as J. J. Chapman said, 'the whole history of America after the Civil War was the story of a railroad passing though a town, and then dominating it.' The American ethos itself was shaped in this period by the lives and attitudes of the robber barons who lived by what James called 'the main American formula' – 'to make so much money that you won't, that you don't mind, don't mind anything.' Apart from the more obvious hypocrisies of those engaged in business who believed themselves to be promoting God's work there was also a movement to make what Henry Adams called 'Caesarism in business' intellectually respectable by invoking the Emersonian doctrine of self-reliance, but the majority of scholars remained steadfastly inimical to the monopolistic corporations and the men who manipulated them throughout the Gilded Age – Thorstein Veblen's enquiry into the life history of material civilization, *The Theory of the Leisure Class*, being perhaps the most obvious example. The industrial revolution provoked a rush of novels too – at least sixty before 1900 dealing with business and business men – most of them criticizing the way of life of the new plutocracy. W. D. Howells came to abhor civilization altogether, feeling that it was turning out all wrong. His gloom is shared by Henry Adams, whose 'melancholy outpouring' drew from James his famous passionate avowal in his continuing interest in life:

> Of course we are lone survivors, of course the past that was our lives is at the bottom of an abyss – if the abyss has any bottom; of course, too, there's no use talking unless one particularly wants to. But the purpose, almost, of my printed divagations was to show you that one can, strange to say, still, want to – or can at least behave as if one did . . . . You see I still, in the presence of life (or of what you deny to be such) have reactions – as many as possible – and the book I send you is a proof of them. It's, I suppose, because I am that queer monster, the artist, an obstinate finality, an inexhaustible sensibility. Hence the reactions – appearances, memories, many things, go on playing upon it with consequences that I note and 'enjoy' (grim word) noting. It all takes doing – and I do. I believe I shall do it yet again – it is still an act of life. (*Letters*, II, 373–4)

This is not to say, of course, that James, any more than Howells or Adams, was satisfied with the shape civilization in America was taking. Though their criteria for judging society appear different, these differences are to a large extent superficial, and what they all three found repugnant in 1900 was the substitution in every branch of American life of so much that was crude and ugly for what had been in their eyes vital, beautiful and noble. In 1868 Adams was full of enthusiasm for the new forces shaping American life. The crudities were yet to come, and though the country needed ornament, 'it needed energy still more, and capital most of all.' Arriving in New York in 1905, his thoughts were very different:

> The outline of the city became frantic in its effort to explain something that defied meaning. Power seemed to have outgrown its servitude and to have asserted its freedom. The cylinder had exploded, and thrown great masses of stone and steam against the sky. The city had the air and movement of hysteria, and the citizens were crying, in every accent of anger and alarm, that the new forces must at any cost be brought under control. Prosperity never before imagined, power never yet wielded by man, speed never reached by anything but a meteor, had made the world irritable, nervous, querulous, unreasonable and afraid. All New York was demanding new men, and all the new forces, condensed into corporations,

were demanding a new type of man – a man with ten times the endurance, energy, will and mind of the old type – for whom they were ready to pay millions at sight. As one jetted over the pavements or read the last week's newspapers, the new man seemed close at hand, for the old man had plainly reached the end of his strength, and his failure had become catastrophic. Everyone saw it, and every municipal election shrieked chaos. A traveller in the highways of history looked out of the club window on the turmoil of Fifth Avenue, and felt himself in Rome, under Diocletian, witnessing the anarchy, conscious of the compulsion, eager for the solution, but unable to conceive whence the next impulse was to come or how it was to act. The two-thousand-years-failure of Christianity roared upward from Broadway and no Constantine the Great was in sight.[1]

James like Veblen before him was concerned primarily with the leisure class, and in a way their books, *The American Scene* and *The Theory of the Leisure Class* provide useful antidotes to one another. While James laments the lack of slowly evolved forms and interests himself in the American attempt to provide for them, Veblen launches a bitter satire on the absurdity of leisure-class institutions: Pecuniary Emulation, Conspicuous Leisure, Conspicuous Consumption, and traces them to their source in the predatory habits and attitudes fostered by a life of acquisition. The fact that Veblen's book appeared in America rather than anywhere else is itself indicative of the barbarism of the Gilded Age. The problem presents itself characteristically to James immediately on his arrival. He had taken a boat out to New Jersey and driven by a chain of large villas stretched tight like a row of 'monstrous pearls':

> The huge new houses, up and down, looked over their smart, short lawns as with a certain familiar prominence in their profiles, which was borne out by the accent, loud, assertive, yet benevolent withal, with which they confessed to their extreme expensiveness. 'Oh yes; we are awfully dear, for what we are and for what we do.' (8)

Unerringly he exposes the general condition responsible for the single ugly symptom:

> Here was the expensive as a power by itself, a power unguided, undirected, practically unapplied, really exerting itself in a void that could make it no response. (9)

He wonders about the people who had erected the villas:

> What had it been their idea to do, the good people – do exactly for their manners, their habits, their intercourse, their relations, their pleasures, their general advantage and justification? Do, that is, in affirming their wealth with such innocent emphasis and yet not at the same time affirming anything else. (10–11)

1. *The Education of Henry Adams* (London, 1928).

It had been their intention to arrive at their goal by way of the 'short-cut'; that is to buy themselves a national culture and a way of life:

The very *donné* of the piece would be given, the subject formulated: the great adventure of a society reaching out into the apparent void for the amenities, the consummations, after having earnestly gathered in so many of the preparations and necessities . . . . Never would there be such a chance to see how the short-cut works, and if there be really any substitute for roundabout experience, for troublesome history, for the long unmitigable process of time. It was a promise, clearly of the highest entertainment. (12–13)

He defers the promised entertainment though, with an extended sojourn among the woods and mountains of New England where the interest was not of the sort 'that involved a consideration of the millions spent'. Here he could dwell on the scenic or pictorial values and cultivate his happier memories of the Lowells, Emerson and Howells. But eventually he had to come to terms with the new, and Chapters 2 to 5 are concerned solely with his impressions of New York – a 'steel-souled, monstrous organism' confronting him with its tremendous energy and vitality and speaking to him always of the interested passions which raised it. Compared with the American skyscraper he finds Giotto's bell-tower in Florence 'serene in its beauty': 'Beauty has been the object of its creator's ideals, and, having found beauty, it has found the form in which it splendidly rests.' The operative word for James here is 'rests'. The tall buildings of New York 'have confessedly arisen but to be "picked" in time, with a shears . . . . Crowned not only with no history, but with no credible possibility of time for history, and consecrated by no uses save the commercial at any cost, they are simply the most piercing notes in a concert of the expensively provisional into which your supreme sense of New York resolves itself . . . . One story is good only till another is told, and skyscrapers are the last word of economic ingenuity only until another word be written.'

The few 'rescued identities' and 'preserved felicities' – Washington Square, the City Hall and Trinity Church – were not sufficient to redeem the 'terrible town' from its mercenary ugliness, reflecting the 'movement of a breathless civilization'. Buildings in James's writings are made to carry a heavy weight of meaning and he obviously believed like Lewis Mumford that 'Architecture, like judgemnt, is about as good as a community deserves. The shell that we create for ourselves marks our spiritual development as plainly as that of a snail denotes its species.'

How much he wanted to find evidence of a maturing civilization here may be judged from his momentary thrill on returning from the

far West when he had the 'absurdest sense of meeting again a ripe old
civilization that showed the mark of established manners', and the
subsequent drop when he reflects that 'the moral was yet once more
that values of a certain order, are, in such conditions, all relative, and
that, as some wants of the spirit must somehow be met, one knocks
together any substitute that will fairly stay the appetite.' The city
(and I dwell on New York, as James did, because although it alone
demonstrated fully in 1904 the manifestations of the new wealth it
was symbolic of the whole continent, and destined anyway to lose its
unique character as capital was diffused throughout the country)
struck from him a note of overwhelming sadness. 'The whole costly
up-town demostration' was, he concluded, 'a record, in the last
analysis, of individual loneliness', and where he had once hoped that
certain American impressions may represent new forms of old
sensibilities, he now came sadly to the conclusion that more often
they represented the absolute extinction of them. Where they do
exist – the old sensibilities, which find in old societies and new
aristocracies expression in 'functions, forms, the whole element of
custom and perpetuity', they fail to find embodiment in the 'consecrated forms' associated with Europe; and James's last criticism is
directed at the general unconsciousness and indifference. He is
returning by train from the South, and in the monotonous rumble of
the pullman's wheels he imagines he can hear a voice forever saying:
'See what I'm making of all this – see what I'm making, what I'm
making.' His answer to this, which occurs at the very end of the
book, may be taken as a final summing up of his American
inpressions:

> I see what you are not making, oh, what you are ever so vividly not
> . . . what strikes me is the long list of the arrears of your undone; and so
> constantly, right and left, that your pretended message of civilization is
> but a colossal recipe for the creation of arrears, and of such as can but
> remain for ever out of hand. You touch the great lonely land – as one feels
> it still to be – only to plant upon it some ugliness about which, never
> dreaming of the grace of apology or contrition, you then proceed to brag
> with a cynicism all your own. You convert the large and noble sanities that
> I see around me, you convert them one after the other to crudities, to
> invalidities, hideous and unashamed. (463–4)

James of course dealt with many other aspects of American life.
He visited the South, wrote about the influx of immigrants on Ellis
Island, listened amazed to the tortured accents of the average
American, and altogether amassed a wealth of evidence testifying to
the fact that he *had* cared and *had* understood. It is not without
justice that he termed himself a 'restless analyst' – every appearance
is probed for its meaning, and sometimes, nurtured by his imagination, these gathered meanings take form in his later fiction. So that

when he wanted a background for his convalescent hero in 'A Round of Visits', he recreated the 'prodigious public setting' of the Waldorf Astoria – 'a temple builded with clustering shrines and chapels, to an idea – a symbol to the supremely gregarious State.' Here his hero can be denied the luxury of 'constituted privacy', and at the same time be forced back on a loneliness which is only emphasized by the life of the huge hotel:

> Passing from one extraordinary masquerade of expensive objects, one portentous 'period' of decoration, one violent phase of publicity to another: the heavy heat, the luxuriance, the extravagance, the quantity, the colour, gave the impression of some wondrous tropical forest, where vociferous, bright-eyed and feathered creatures of every variety of size and hue, were half smothered between undergrowths of velvet and tapestry and ramifications of marble and bronze. The fauna and the flora startled him alike, and among them his bruised spirit drew in and folded its wings. (12)

Similarly in 'The Jolly Corner', Spencer Brydon feels all the nostalgia for old New York that James had and the ugliness of life in the sprawling modern city is symbolized by the ugliness of the apparition of what Brydon himself would have become had he remained there instead of passing his life in Europe. James's travels in America served him best, though, when he came to write *The Ivory Tower*. He chose for its setting Newport, a town he had known intimately from his earliest years and which he had revisited in 1904. It was a good choice. Newport was a necessary adjunct to New York and James found that it gave 'supreme support' to his reading of the conditions of New York opulence.

In 1870 he had found Newport 'substantial' and 'civilized': 'The villas and cottages, the beautiful idle women, the beautiful idle men, the brilliant pleasure-fraught days and evenings, impart, perhaps, to Newport life a faintly European expression, insofar as they suggest the somewhat alien presence of leisure.' 'Nowhere', he found, 'within the range of our better civilization – does business seem so remote, so vague and unreal.' His infatuation leads him to speculate on the tenants who occupy the summer villas, and he comes up with a passage which contrasts markedly with parallel descriptions in *The Ivory Tower*:

> How sensible they ought to be, the denizens of these pleasant places, of their peculiar felicity and distinction! How it should purify their temper and refine their tastes! How delicate, how wise, how discriminating they should become! What excellent manners – what enlightened opinion – their situation should produce! How it should purge them of vulgarity! Happy *villeggianti* of Newport. (*American Scene*, 490)

On revisiting Newport he remembered his early infatuation and pictures the early town as a small white hand which, during his

absence, has had heaped into it things of an ugly and expensive sort –
gold 'of an amount so oddly out of proportion to the scale of nature
and of sapce,' He attempts to catch the tone of Newport as it was
before it was weighed down beneath the 'palpable pile', but again
and again he is forced back upon the 'multiplied excrescencies' –
symbols of the 'great black ebony god of business' – with which
Newport has been covered. These 'white elephants', as he calls
them, 'pure and conscious and humpish – some of them as with an
air of the brandished proboscis, – really grotesque', together with
'cars and telephones and facilities and machineries' provide him with
his properties in *The Ivory Tower*. And he felt very stongly the need
for such properties to help in over-coming the enormous difficulties
he encountered with the book – the chief one being that of
'pretending to show various things here as with a business vision, in
my total absence of business initiation.'[2] James, one must conclude,
underestimated his ability to evoke the atmosphere. It is true that he
had no knowledge at all of Wall Street or the great corporations –
those complexities did elude him – but what he understood so well
was the society which could produce or be produced by these
phenomena: the millionaires and their parasites passing their brief
season in the new, disfigured Newport. Even here, he felt, he was
violating verismilitude; for the Newport era was in truth finished,
and his protagonists were more likely at this late day to be found in
Paris. But James recognized the need for an American setting and
Newport, as I have said, was the perfect choice carrying as it did 'the
chink of money itself in the murmur of the breezy little waves at the
foot of the cliff.'

Here, in two adjacent, over-ornamented, ugly villas, two old rival
millionaires have come to pass the season, and to die. One – Abel
Gaw, the richer of the two – lives on for the sole purpose of out-living
the other, Frank Betterman, and to discover the extent of his
fortune. In superb prose, economical yet fluid, James presents the
concomitants, in terms of human personality, of the 'abysses of New
York financial history', which, while never actually intruding,
occupies the periphery of the novel's action. Abel Gaw is the epitome
of the machine age; predatory, ruthless, and ugly, he perches on
Betterman's veranda: 'like a ruffled-hawk, motionless but for his
single tremor, with his beak, which had pecked so many hearts out,
visibly sharper than ever, yet only his talons nervous.' Into his
portrait of the old man James gathers up all his hatred of the type:

> He was a person without an alternative, and if any had ever been open to
> him, at an odd hour or two, somewhere in his inner dimness, he had long
> since closed the gates against it and now revolved in the hard-rimmed

2. See his Notes for *The Ivory Tower* (London, 1927).

circle from which he had not a single issue. You couldn't retire without something or somewhere to retire to. You must have planted a single tree at least for shade or be able to turn a key in some yielding door; but to say that her extraordinary parent was surrounded by the desert was almost to flatter the void into which he invited one to step.(4)

James had always known, obviously, of the existence of such men as Gaw, and had attempted relatively unsuccessful portrayals of them in *The Portrait of a Lady, The American* and *The Golden Bowl*. What must have struck him though, as an absolutely new feature of the scene, were the hordes of sycophantic socialites – 'all laughter and shimmer, all senseless sound and expensive futility',21 who made up the summer population. New, that is to say, in America. Cissy Foy and Haughty Vint are very close to being recreations of Kate Croy and Merton Densher, and the fact that the swindle perpetrated by the Europeans, Kate and Densher, is on an American whereas it is the Europeanized Gray Fielder who is victimized in *The Ivory Tower*, should make us aware of James's growing doubts regarding the moral superiority of Americans. It is true that Rosanna Gaw, with her fine discriminations against the dollar civilization, is an American, but she is presented as distinctly untypical. (It is she, we remember, who, at a critical time urges Fielder to remain in Europe rather than return to America to be apprenticed to the 'game of grab'.) The typical product of American civilization, insofar as the typical ever finds expression in James's work, is Gussy Bradham. Vulgar, stupid, and loud, she is very much the 'terrible woman of the future'. This in reality is what has become of the American Girl, Daisy Miller; brutalized, changed almost beyond recognition, her career parallels and reflects the changed American ethos and James deals with her at some length:

> With her wondrous bloom of life and health and her hard confidence that had nothing to do with sympathy . . . her braveries of aspect and attitude, resources of resistance to time and thought, things not of beauty, for some unyielding reason, and quite as little of dignity, but things of assertion and application in an extraordinary degree, things of a straight cold radiance and of an emphasis that was like the stamp of hard flat feet. (47–8)

These then are the people, recognizably akin to the object of Veblen's mordant, sardonic satire, whom James chooses to represent the new American sensibility.

Following the typical pattern, but with the usual values reversed he projects into the midst of this rapacious crew his 'innocent', Gray Fielder. Fielder is an American too, the nephew of Frank Betterman, but he has been brought up in Europe, and in his Notes James is quite definite about the type he wanted. He is to be:

> an anomaly and an outsider alike in the New York world of business, the

NY world of ferocious acquistion, and the world there of enormities of expenditure and extravagance, so that the real suppression for him of anything that shall count in the American air as a money-making, or even as a wage-earning, or as a pecuniary-picking-up character, strikes me as wanted for my emphasis of his entire difference of sensibility and association . . .. Yet I want something as different as possible, no less different, I mean, from the people who are 'idle' there than from the people who are active.

Brought to America by the impending death of his uncle, he discovers that he has inherited Betterman's fortune; the old man at the end of his life having finally realized the emptiness of the business world has now made provision to avoid the bolstering up of a system 'so full of poison'. Thus Fielder is prepared for the descent of the vultures, and the action of the novel as first planned in the Notes, consists of the swindle perpetrated by Haughty Vint, and the effect it would have on Gray's 'moral nerves' and 'reflective imagination'. As James came more to grips with his problem in the Notes, however, he saw that this outline would not carry the weight of criticism he intended to load it with. A simple story of fraud was not at all what he wanted, and though he rejected his former plan on the grounds that it would harm the envisaged moral complexity of Haughty, it is significant that it also fails to allow him to treat adequately the money world itself. He felt that he wanted something more 'for the process by which my young man works off the distress, his distaste for the ugliness of his inheritance', and he writes a speech in which Haughty pinpoints for Gray the cause of his malaise:

> 'You mind, in you extraordinary way, how this money was accumulated and hanky-pankied, you suffer, and cultivate a suffering, from the perpetrated wrong of which you feel it the embodied evidence, and with which the possession of it is thereby poisoned for you.' (333)

The real tragedy for Fielder comes when he realizes that the 'blank cheque' signed by Mr Betterman will not be honoured – morally, that is, not legally. The great advantage for him had been 'much less in the fact that he could lisp in dollars, as it were, and see the dollars come, than in those vast vague quantities, those spreading tracts, of his own consciousness itself on which his kinsman's prodigious perversity had imposed, as for his exploration, the aspect of a boundless capital.' He sees himself distributing his money 'after the fashion of Rockefellers and their like', but he is brought up sharp by Rosanna, who puts it to him that their funds (she has inherited 20 millions from *her* father, and 'loathes every separate dollar of it') 'are so dishonoured and stained and blackened at their very roots, that it seems to her that they carry their curse with them, and that she asks herself what application to "benevolence" as commonly understood, can purge them, can make them anything but continuators, some-how or other, of the wrongs in which they had their origin.' In such ways as this Gray comes to see what 'black and merciless things are behind the great possessions', and his 'rising disgusts' culminate in a symbolic renunciation of America as they return to the richer life of Europe.

It may seem to us now that the success of the American industrial revolution was finally assured in the last quarter of the nineteenth century; and indeed Toynbee gives 1870 as the year in which it first became apparent that the revolution in Britain was not just an isolated phenomenon. Yet the attendant political, intellectual and literary crises did not make themselves felt until much later. Most historians agree that James was writing *The Ivory Tower* at a time which formed the turning point in America's history:

> In the second decade of the twentieth century the nation faced a crisis in the conflict of forces within itself that had first declared themselves in the 1890s, and creative energies were released, with their doubts as well as their confidence, into literature and criticism. The outlines of that conflict had by then emerged clearly and even boldly. On the one side lay an America predominantly agrarian, concerned with domestic problems, conforming – intellectually at least – to the political, economic and moral principles inherited from the eighteenth century; an America still in the making, physically and politically, an America on the whole self-confident, self-contained, and conscious of its unique character and of a unique destiny. On the other side lay the modern America, predominantly urban and industrial, inextricably involved in world economics and politics, troubled with the social and economic problems that had been long thought peculiarly the burden of the Old World, desperately trying to accommodate its traditional institutions and habits of thought to conditions new and in part alien.[3]

This dichotomy crystallized into warring groups of political reformers. But James, thinking more radically than the politicians, or than the muck-raking novelists of a later generation, realized that the way of life celebrated in *The Europeans* – 'The eighteenth century priciples' – could not be revived. Nor, he saw, did the Americans seem very successful in accommodating traditional institutions to new conditions. The bleak, pessimistic vision of life in *The Ivory Tower* must stand as his last prophecy about America. For himself, he elected to spend his remaining time in a symbolic but futile effort to help preserve English and French civilization from a different and more violent form of barbarism. His death in 1916 coincided exactly with the end of an era.

3. *Literary History of the United States*, ed. by R. E. Spiller, W. Thorpe, T. H. Johnson and H. S. Canby (New York, 1948).

Bibliographical Note

Page references in the text are to the following editions of James's novels and stories:

Collins, London

 The Ivory Tower (1917)

John Lehmann, London

 The Bostonians (1952), The Europeans (1952), The Lesson of the Master, and other stories (1948), Washington Square (1951), What Maisie Knew (1947).

Macmillan, London, 1921–23

 The Altar of the Dead, and other Tales (1922), The Ambassadors (1923), The American (1879) The Awkward Age (1922), Daisy Miller (1922), The Golden Bowl (1923), The Princess Casamassima (1921), Roderick Hudson (1921), The Sacred Fount (1923), The Spoils of Poynton (1921), The Wings of the Dove (1923).

Oxford University Press, London

 The Portrait of a Lady (1947)

Rupert Hart-Davis, London

 The Tragic Muse (1948)

Scribner, New York

 The Finer Grain (1910)

Further Reading

Leon Edel's five volume biography of Henry James, (*The Untried Years (1843–1870), The Conquest of London (1870–1881), The Middle Years (1882–1895), The Treacherous Years (1895–1901, The Master (1901–1916)*) should be read in conjuction with James's three volume autobiography (*A Small Boy and Others, Notes of a Son and Brother, The Middle Years*). Edel's work is published by J. B. Lippincott in the USA. and by Rupert Hart-Davis in England. There is also a two-volume edition published by Penguin Books, 1978. The *Autobiography* is available in a single volume (W. H. Allen, 1956). Invaluable help for those wishing to trace further James's relation to his father's and brother's thought is provided by F. O. Matthiessen's *The James Family* (Knopf, 1948) and Hartley Grattan's *The Three Jameses: A Family of Minds* (New York University Press, 1962). Richard A. Hocks also studies the relationship between William James's philosophy and his brother's fiction in *Henry James and Pragmatistic Thought* (University of North Carolina Press, 1974).

James's scattered writings on the novel have been collected and arranged by James E. Miller, Jr in *Theory of Fiction: Henry James* (University of Nebraska Press, 1972), and his critical prefaces to the New York edition of the novels by R. P. Blackmur in *The Art of the Novel* (Scribner's, 1934). *The Notebooks of Henry James*, edited by F. O. Matthiessen and K. B. Murdock (Oxford University Press, 1961) provide fascinating clues to his sources and the development of his technique,

Oscar Cargill's study, *The Novels of Henry James* (Macmillan, 1961), as well as giving a lucid critical account of the novels, provides a wealth of interesting documentation about their sources, development and reception. There is also an excellent collection of contemporary reviews and essays available in Roger Gard's *Henry James: The Critical Heritage* (Routledge and Kegan Paul, Barnes and Noble, 1968).

Index